THE GOLDEN AGE OF PLAYER DEVELOPMENT

A Guide to Foundation Phase Coaching

Rob Porter

Oakamoor Publishing

Published in 2025 by Oakamoor Publishing, an imprint of Bennion Kearny Ltd

Woodside, Oakamoor, ST10 3AE, UK

www.bennionkearny.com

ISBN: 978-1-910773-94-9

Rob Porter has asserted his right under the Copyright, Designs and Patents Act, 1988, to be identified as the author of this book.

Copyright Rob Porter 2025. All Rights Reserved.

No part of this publication may be reproduced, stored in a retrieval system, or transmitted in any form or by any means, electronic, mechanical, photocopying, recording or otherwise, without the prior permission of the publisher.

A CIP catalogue record for this book is available from the British Library.

This book is sold subject to the condition that it shall not, by way of trade or otherwise, be lent, re-sold, hired out or otherwise circulated without the publisher's prior consent in any form of binding or cover other than that in which it is published and without a similar condition including this condition being imposed on the subsequent purchaser.

Oakamoor Publishing is an imprint of Bennion Kearny Limited. 6 Woodside, Churnet View Road, Oakamoor, ST10 3AE, United Kingdom.

Acknowledgements

A massive thank you to my wife, Katie, and my sons, Liam and Hayden, for spending countless hours listening to me talk about football, coaching, and this book while I've been writing it. Not everyone would put up with me!

A big thank you to Peter Thornton, who was an amazing help with the book writing process.

Also, a big thank you to James Lumsden-Cook for taking a chance on me as a first-time author, believing in this book, and helping turn it into the finished book.

About The Author

Rob Porter is a coach with over 10 years of experience working in a range of different environments. Rob has worked for Oxford United for the past 7 years, with both the Community programme, where he went full-time in 2023 as the Lead community coach, and the Girls Academy, where he has coached every age group and served as the Foundation Phase lead. He has also worked in the grassroots game, coaching both of his sons from the Foundation Phase until U17s.

Rob has gained his UEFA B licence, as well as his FA Youth award, after completing all three modules and the National Goalkeeper course.

Coach development

Alongside his coaching roles, Rob works for the FA as the Women and Girls Community Champion for Oxfordshire and for the Oxfordshire FA as an FA-approved CPD tutor. Rob also delivers the FA Developing Leadership through Football award in a prison environment in association with the Twinning Project.

Coaching variety

Rob has worked with every age group throughout the Foundation and Youth Development Phases in Grassroots, Development Centre, and Academy environments. He has also worked with 5-to-13-year-olds in after-school clubs and holiday camp settings.

Contents

Foreword 1

1: Creating the Environment 2

2: Helping Your Players Develop 13

3: Coaching Factors 25

4: Practice Considerations 42

5: Practices 58
    How to view these practices 58
    Ball Mastery 59
    Traffic Lights 60
    King of the Ring 62
    Gates Game 63
    The Stadium Game 65
    Skills Corridor 66
    Tag Games 68
    Chicken or Hero 69
    1v1 Tournament 71
    1v1 to Stay on the Ball 72
    Rondos 74

The Zoo Game 75
The Transfer Game 77
Robin Hood 78
Battleships 80
Possession v Pressure 81
Numbers Game 83
Gladiators 84
Finishing Wave Practice 86
Three-Team Finishing 88
Conditioned and other SSGs 89

6: Technical Detail 93

7: Match Days 107

Foreword

The Football Association defines the Foundation Phase in football as the stage for players aged 5 to 11, emphasising the development of fundamental skills, a love for the game, and a strong connection between the player and the ball. This phase prioritises individual ball work, exploring and experimenting with new techniques, and developing a positive attitude towards the sport.

The Foundation Phase is the golden age of learning and the time when, as coaches, we can instil a lifelong love for the game if we create positive experiences for the players we coach.

The Foundation Phase, for me, is the most important phase in player development; the time when you lay the foundation for all their future knowledge to be built on. But it's the area that tends to be the most neglected in the coaching community. With a lot of coaches, there tends to be a race to the top, to get to the older age groups or adult football, where coaching most represents the game that they see on TV.

I want to use this book to share my views on the Foundation Phase, which I have built on my experiences working in grassroots, development centre, and academy environments. The aim is to give coaches working in the Foundation Phase a handy resource that they can use. At the same time, I believe the contents would also apply to most ages and environments.

1: Creating the Environment

> " Young players need freedom of expression to develop as creative players. They should be encouraged to try skills without fear of failure.
>
> **Arsene Wenger**

Why is creating the environment important?

Creating a positive environment is where everything begins because it develops a sense of belonging, and encourages risk-taking and development. It leads to improved performances and enjoyment of the game. It allows players to make mistakes without fear of judgment, creating a growth mindset where setbacks are viewed as opportunities for learning and improvement.

During this chapter, we will look at how you can develop a positive environment for your Foundation Phase group.

Making enjoyment a priority

The key to a successful environment is *enjoyment*. Young players don't want to turn up to sessions that are going to be boring. By making sessions enjoyable, players go home happy, which – in turn – leads to players being excited to go to training sessions, which then has a positive impact at the start of sessions. It becomes a positive cycle, which makes the rest of your coaching easier.

On my UEFA B licence coaching course, I was lucky enough to have Des Buckingham (Former New Zealand U23s and Oxford

United manager) as my tutor. During my end-of-course presentation, he asked whether every session should be enjoyable (as I had said that enjoyment was one of my priorities in my coaching philosophy). I paused for a minute, a little puzzled about how to answer, as I thought it might be a trick question!

Eventually, I answered yes. I told him that I believed every session should be enjoyable. He smiled and told me he was glad I'd said that, as I valued it so highly.

Whether we are running Foundation Phase, grassroots, development centre, academy, wildcats or social inclusion sessions, players' enjoyment should be at the *forefront* of our minds.

The best sessions with Foundation Phase players tend to be the ones where the players are enjoying themselves so much that they hardly notice our coaching.

If we want your players to keep coming back, make enjoyment a priority.

A great way to think about your environment

When a flower doesn't grow, you fix the environment in which it grows, not the plant.

**Alexander den Heijer,
Dutch inspirational speaker**

This Alexander den Heijer quote perfectly sums up the mindset we should have about our environments.

In the past, when I was a younger coach, I was guilty of getting frustrated with players who were messing around or not listening.

When I look back now, I realise it was down to me not creating a good environment for them, using practices that weren't right for them, or talking too much!

Always look inward and see what we could do differently before blaming our players.

It's easy to blame our players when things go wrong, but it's important to look at ourselves and our environment first.

More often than not, the misbehaviour of players is usually down to what we are (or are not) doing.

Create an environment where players grow!

The reason why enjoyment is important

 We learn best in moments of enjoyment.

Ralph C Smedley, Founder of Toastmasters International

Setting standards

We want players to enjoy themselves in our sessions, but that can't be at the expense of learning and behaviour. By setting standards early, players will understand what is expected of them.

Getting players to buy into the team or club's standards can then lead to gentle reminders of the standards that are expected of them, which help to maintain the standards we set. Setting high standards can lead to a really positive environment. Standards can include:

- Representing the badge. We should encourage our players to be the best possible versions of themselves when wearing a top with the club badge. Create a feeling of being proud to wear the club badge.

- Being polite. Most importantly being polite to each other as players, but also being polite to people like coaches, match officials, and other parents.

- Hard work. Creating an environment where hard work is valued and expected will help lead players towards having a good work ethic in everything they do. This will stand them in good stead outside football, as well as in a football environment.

- Commitment. In the Foundation Phase, a commitment to turning up is more due to parents than the players, as parents get players to sessions and matches. But if we can set it as a standard early on, it will help when players get older and become less reliant on their parents.

- Treating others with respect. Treating others with respect helps to create a bond between players, which helps on the pitch as well as during sessions.

Setting high standards does not mean being a disciplinarian and shouting at your players. You can set high standards while also being a fun and enthusiastic coach. It's about gentle reminders about standards, and friendly chats when they aren't met.

Now and then, you may need to go a step further and potentially sit a player out for a few minutes or (in very rare cases) have a chat with the player and their parent about standards. But if you are following the steps set out in this book, these situations should be few and far between.

Interacting with parents

Alongside setting standards for our players, setting out standards and our vision with parents is crucial, especially with younger age groups when parents may be new to a sporting environment involving their child.

We always need to remember that parents only want what's best for their children. By setting out what we're trying to achieve and how we are trying to achieve it, we are more likely to get parents on our side. This can help with our coaching, as the parents will be repeating the same messages as we are, and they are less likely to be telling players contrary information or alternative ideas when they are talking to their youngsters away from training.

One of the biggest issues coaches come across is parents shouting instructions from the sidelines, both during training sessions and games. It is done with good intent, as the parent thinks that they are giving a little extra help to their child, but it's detrimental to the player and our coaching.

For a Foundation Phase player, there is a lot going on during a match day. They are already thinking about the ball, their teammates, the opposition, and the coach's instructions. What they don't need is a parent adding to that while they are trying to play.

As coaches, we will give our players objectives before the game, and we can help them during the game, but that will have far less effect if parents are shouting instructions at their kids. What they are communicating could be the opposite of what we want as coaches.

A parents meeting at the start of the season, where we set out exactly what we are trying to achieve, and how we are planning to go about doing it, puts everyone in the loop and gets parents on the same page as ourselves. It will also help parents to understand what is expected from them on a match day (e.g., to encourage their children but not to shout instructions, and to let the coaches coach).

What we can include in a parents meeting

- How parents can assist the coach on training nights (getting their children there early, communicating beforehand if they will be late or unable to attend)

- Ways that parents can assist on match days (sorting nets, being an assistant referee, corner flags, etc.)

- The coach's coaching philosophy (we will cover this later in the book)

- Team standards

- How you, as the coach, plan to communicate logistical information

- Sidelines standards

Communicating with parents

A solid level of communication with parents can really help us as coaches. Letting everyone know *ahead of time* when and where training is, as well as match day logistics, makes everything a lot smoother than leaving it to the last minute.

The traditional way of doing it is to put all of the parents into a WhatsApp group and send the required information on there. The issue with that tends to be getting parents to respond, so it's hard to know how many players we will have at training.

Another way to communicate is through an app like Spond or 360 Player, where parents get a notification, and they just have to press a button to let coaches know about attending training and games.

Connecting with the person as well as the player

Good coaching isn't just about improving a player's ability on the pitch. By connecting with players – as people – it helps them feel more valued and helps them buy into our coaching, as well as the environment that we are building.

How do you build a connection with your players?

It's as simple as asking questions! Getting to know things like their favourite football team, favourite player, pets, siblings, etc.

Start by asking questions *before* sessions commence, such as, "How has your day been?" or "How was school today?" Not only does this make players feel like we care about them (which we should!), but it also helps us gauge their mood before sessions, which will give us an idea of how they feel.

Another key to connecting with players is following up on the questions you ask. If we ask a player what they are doing at the weekend, and they say they are going to the zoo, then ask them how the zoo was at the start of the next session.

Something as small as the above shows players that not only have we asked them a question about themselves, but we have listened and remembered it. That is very powerful.

People don't care how much you know, until they know how much you care.

Theodore Roosevelt, 26th President of the United States

Getting down to the players' level

As an adult coach in the Foundation Phase, we may be double the height and maybe three times the weight of the players we're coaching. If we are towering over them, it can be quite intimidating!

By getting down to the players' level, we feel less intimidating to them, and it means we can have good eye contact with the players at the same level.

Sometimes, the simple things can make a big impact.

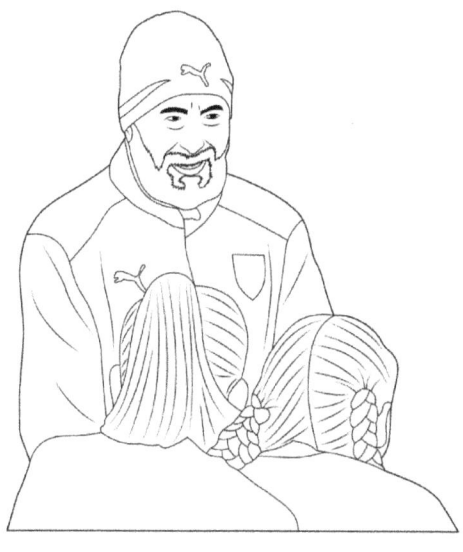

Interacting with players outside of a football setting

Getting out of a football environment from time to time can greatly help our coaching environment. Having players interacting with each other and coaches *without footballs being involved* (apart from footgolf!) is very beneficial.

If we do something like bowling, and we don't want to take part (i.e., bowl ourselves), it can be a great time to interact with parents and get to know them.

Remember, though, that youngsters are our players, not our friends, and we need to keep boundaries.

Positivity and enthusiasm

We can't expect to create a positive environment if we are negative as coaches. Even the youngest players can pick up on negative body language, let alone negative interactions.

If we go into sessions and match days with a positive mindset and an enthusiastic attitude, it will rub off on players. If, on the other hand, we are negative towards players, they are more likely to be negative and defensive around us.

Something as simple as a smile and a fist bump or high five at the start of a session, or when players arrive on a match day, is such a small thing, but it can have a massive positive impact on young players.

I've been lucky enough to see lots of different environments over the years, and for me, the best ones have been where the coach is full of energy, as well as positivity and enthusiasm.

Chris Ramsey, who is technical director at QPR, said that a Foundation Phase coach should be Ronald McDonald in Copas, which I think is a great quote and neatly captures the kind of positivity that coaches should bring.

I'm sure that if you think back to your school days or your playing days, the teachers or coaches who were positive and enthusiastic were the ones that you remember most fondly.

Being a positive role model to your players

As coaches, we are in an enviable position, as most players enjoy being in a football environment more than school! We can become role models who then have a massively positive impact on them, both as a person and as a player.

Being a positive role model isn't just about how we talk to players and what we say. Being a positive role model is also about the example we set.

If we turn up late, we aren't reliable, or we speak to opposition coaches and officials disrespectfully, it will rub off on our players. So, think about how players view *your* actions.

Safeguarding your players

At a minimum, players should be able to turn up and be safe during sessions and matches.

The training sessions and match days that we have with our players may well be the highlight of their week, and it could be their chance to get away from the problems they experience away from the pitch.

Most of our players will be in good situations, but we have a safeguarding responsibility to them, and if we see signs that we don't think are right, we shouldn't ignore them.

Make sure that we know the proper channels to report any safeguarding issues to, and make sure that we report safeguarding issues. We need to make sure that everyone is safe in our care.

2: Helping Your Players Develop

> " You build a player like you build a house.
> You start with the fundamentals. "
>
> **Arsene Wenger**

Building the foundations

The Foundation Phase is all about building up a technical and physical base. Basic techniques and the ABCS (Agility, Balance, Coordination and Speed) should be a priority over formations and tactics. It doesn't matter if a player understands a high press if they struggle with movement skills or controlling a football!

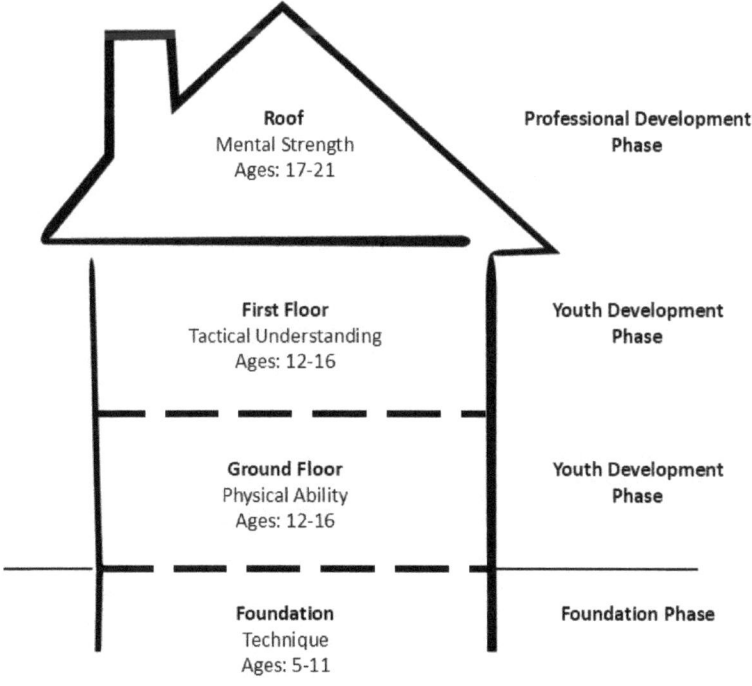

Developing players to play in different positions

We may think that our U7 centre-back is the next John Stones or Millie Bright, but once they have finished growing, they could end up being the smallest player on the team! So, pigeonholing them early may have a detrimental effect.

Giving players experiences in different positions helps them to develop a more rounded skillset. The game is completely different across positions. A full-back, for example, tends to have the sideline close to them, whilst a centre-midfielder has an entirely different set of challenges.

A more well-rounded player will be able to adapt to different situations and different formations once they get into the Youth Development phase and beyond.

Getting players to fall in love with the ball

For players to fall in love with the ball, they need to spend lots of time with a ball, and they need a coach who is happy for them to make mistakes on the ball. If players get shouted at every time they lose the ball, they won't want to have the ball.

Having worked in lots of different environments, it's always clear when I see players who have not mastered the ball. When they receive it, it's like a hot potato, and they want to get rid of it!

Do lots of ball mastery and practice where there is a ball per player, pair, or small group. This will help players gain confidence on the ball.

Teaching scanning and spatial awareness

The best players in the game scan regularly. Frank Lampard was recorded moving his head and scanning 0.62 times per second. In other words, for almost 37 seconds in every minute of playing time, Lampard was looking around to understand where everyone was on the pitch. Scanning is basically information gathering.

Getting our players to scan regularly will slow the game down for them, as they can make decisions before receiving the ball, rather than after receiving it. They will understand what is around them before the ball is at their feet, which allows them to make quicker decisions.

As well as the act of scanning, getting players to understand what they are scanning for is important. A player who scans regularly will understand where their teammates and opposition players are, but they will also understand the space they are in, and where there is space to play.

Working on players' non-dominant feet

One of the biggest advantages we can give players in the Foundation Phase is the ability to be comfortable using both feet so that a player's non-dominant foot isn't only for standing on!

Getting Foundation Phase players to work on using both feet will help them become far more effective both in possession and out of possession, especially when keeping the ball under pressure, and keeping the ball on the safe side when dribbling.

Some of the best players of all time have the ability to pass, receive, beat players, and score goals with both feet. It is an area that players will struggle with initially, but persevering with it will benefit players in the long term. Developing players with two feet will take time, but it is a must in the modern game.

Dominating 1v1 situations

Developing players who can dominate in 1v1 situations – both in possession and out of possession – will create better-rounded players who are able to win their 1v1 battles on the pitch.

Just because we think someone is a striker, it doesn't mean that their ability to defend 1v1 isn't important, and just because we think someone is a defender, it doesn't mean that their ability to beat a player 1v1 isn't a valuable asset to both themselves and the team.

Some players may think that working on defending is boring, but a defending session still needs players to attack; it's just a different focus. Telling players that they will get exactly the same number of chances to attack in a defending session usually helps with buy-in.

Encouraging practice away from training

Although we – as coaches – probably have the biggest impact on our players' development, how fast players develop isn't all down to us. Players who practise away from sessions and matches have an advantage over those who don't.

Especially in the Foundation Phase, players may only get one hour a week of training time and a 40-minute match at the weekend. Encouraging players to practise at home can be very beneficial if we want players to develop.

Although we can encourage players to practise at home, some players are happy with just practice at training and matches. But if we can get them to *fall in love with the ball*, they are more likely to practise at home.

This doesn't mean players need loads of equipment or to pay for one-to-one sessions. Something as simple as a ball and a wall can be a great benefit to passing and receiving. A wall never gets bored, and it never gets tired!

Some Foundation Phase players will be lucky enough to have parents or siblings who take them out and have a kick about, which is great. And with our parent meetings, we can tell parents about the benefits of practising away from training, which may encourage more parents to practise with their kids.

At the same time, we can also show players ways of developing themselves when they don't have anyone to practise with. Whether it is a ball and a wall, as we have already stated, ball mastery, keep ups, or finishing, as long as they have a safe place to practise, they can improve themselves.

Giving players the freedom to try and fail

If some of the greatest players of all time only complete around 50% of their 1v1s, we can't expect Foundation Phase players to win 1v1s all the time, either.

Keep encouraging players and give them the freedom to keep trying 1v1 moves and turns to beat players, both in training sessions and matches. Eventually, it will help develop creative players.

The Top Ten Dribblers, according to OPTA from 2006 to 2019	
1. Lionel Messi	1,880 take-ons completed (57.2%)
2. Eden Hazard	1,220 take-ons completed (57.1%)

3. Franck Ribery	939 take-ons completed (47.9%)
4. Sergio Aguero	832 take-ons completed (46.6%)
5. Christiano Ronaldo	816 take-ons completed (44%)
6. Joaquin	798 take-ons completed (50.9%)
7. Hatem Ben Arfa	770 take-ons completed (50.6%)
8. Andres Iniesta	739 take-ons completed (60.9%)
9. Roberto Firmino	736 take-ons completed (56.8%)
10. Neymar	734 take-ons completed (50.2%)

Players with the most successful dribbles in 2024/25

Player	Completed	Attempts	Completion percentage
Lamine Yamal	223	404	55%
Vinicius Junior	145	340	43%
Jeremy Doku	140	255	55%
Kylian Mbappe	133	258	52%
Nico Williams	126	301	42%

Player	Completed	Attempts	Completion percentage
Rafael Leao	115	224	51%
Jamal Musiala	112	223	48%
Jamie Gittens	111	223	50%
Florian Wirtz	109	215	51%
Mohammed Kudus	106	206	51%

A great way to look at failing and learning

I was introduced to the saying below, recently, and although it applies to every age group, it is particularly powerful in the Foundation Phase, where players do everything for the first time.

First

Attempt

In

Learning

Let players try and fail. Don't be too quick to correct everything. You will often be surprised at how players will self-correct.

Appropriate language

To state the obvious, in general terms, appropriate language means not swearing at players and having appropriate conversations for children.

From a coaching perspective, appropriate language means using coaching terminology that Foundation Phase players will understand.

It is easy to watch Match of the Day, with pundits talking about pressing structures and inverted full-backs, then take that language and try to use it with our players.

Putting together a vocabulary of words you use with your players can be a game changer; if *everyone* uses and understands your coaching vocabulary it will help Foundation Phase players hugely. The main things to consider would be

- Keep it simple. Young players won't understand and don't need to hear fancy coaching terms. If we talk about Gegenpressing with U7s, it will go over their heads. Remember that they are children, not adults, so make everything as simple as possible.

- Coach the detail behind the words. I have heard many coaches shouting things like 'pass detail' or 'quality of the pass' to their players, but do the players know the detail involved? For me, working with Foundation Phase players, 'pass detail' means accuracy of pass, weight of pass, and no bobble on the pass to feet or space. Make sure that players understand the detail behind the words.

- Young players take everything literally. I remember talking to Peter Thornton, and he said he had watched a Foundation Phase game when the coach shouted 'second ball'. To this, most of the players looked around for a second ball on the pitch!

Foundation Phase players need coaching that is right for their age and understanding. Make everything as simple as possible, and try to support your communication with visual aids like demos and tactics boards to help understanding.

Football terminology explained

When working with Foundation Phase players, you should keep the language you use at an appropriate level for the group you are working with. On TV, as well as coaching articles, podcasts, and webinars, you will hear more complex terminology.

Here are a few of the common terms you will hear and what they mean in the simpler terms that Foundation Phase players will understand. Not all of these will translate to Foundation Phase teams, but they are good to know.

- **In possession:** When we have the ball

- **Out of possession:** When we don't have the ball

- **Transition in:** When we have just won the ball

- **Transition out:** When we have just lost the ball

- **Counter-attack:** When we have just won the ball and look to score quickly

- **Pressing:** When we try to win the ball from the opposition with intensity

- **Counter-press:** When we have just lost the ball and we try to win it back straight away

- **High press:** When we try to play as high as possible up the pitch when we don't have the ball, so that we can win it back near the opposition goal

- **Mid-block:** When we wait for the opposition to get into the middle third of the pitch before we look to win the ball

- **Low-block:** When we defend deep, near to our own box, and let the opposition come to us before trying to win the ball

- **Unit:** Players who play in the same group (Defenders, Midfielders, Attackers)

- **Compact:** When we are close to together in Units, or as a team, when we don't have the ball

- **Width:** The width of the furthest players apart on each side of the pitch

- **Depth:** The depth of the players in the team

- **Switching play:** When we pass the ball from one side of the pitch to the other, trying to find space to play

- **Half-turn:** When we receive the ball with a body shape that means that we can see both goals

- **Back to goal:** When we receive the ball facing our goal, not the opposition's

- **Combination play:** When two or more players in the team combine to move the ball by passing it between each other

- **Breaking lines:** When we pass the ball beyond opposition players

- **Overlap:** When a player makes a forward run on the outside of the player who has the ball

- **Underlap:** When a player makes a forward run on the inside of the player who has the ball

Different learning styles

Research has shown that people (and players, of course) prefer to learn in different ways.

Visual:

- These learners excel when information is presented visually, such as through pictures, videos, laid-out practices, or on a tactics board.

Auditory:

- Auditory learners prefer listening to information, whether through the coach's communication or broader discussions.

Reading/Writing:

- These learners thrive when information is presented in written form, such as through notes or writing on a tactics board.

Kinaesthetic:

- Kinaesthetic learners learn best through demonstrations of practices, walking them through what they need to do.

Developing as a coach will help your players develop, too

To get the best out of our players, we need to invest time in our coaching to develop into the best versions of ourselves.

In the Foundation Phase, time spent on areas like learning about technical detail or learning about 'how children learn' will also be very beneficial to us and our players.

There will be time, later on, when we can do a deep dive into the tactical detail of a high press in a 1-4-3-3 when playing against a 1-3-5-2, but none of that will really benefit our Foundation Phase players right now. What they need is the finer details of completing a flip flap or a solid foundation for their 1v1 defending technique.

Courses, CPD events, books, articles, webinars and podcasts are all great ways to develop ourselves.

When I started coaching, I coached alongside an older coach who was very experienced, and a younger coach who was inexperienced but very eager to learn.

I saw firsthand a coach whose heart was in the right place but who felt that he knew enough, and a coach who took every opportunity to develop themselves, by completing youth modules, attending CPD events, watching other coaches, and reading books.

I saw both sides directly. The experience had a massive impact on me and helped make me the coach I am today.

3: Coaching Factors

> Time spent learning +
> Time spent on the grass +
> Reviewing
> = Becoming a better coach.
>
> **Rob Porter**

The formula for effective coach development

We all follow different paths, but there are elements that we all need to develop ourselves effectively.

Courses are important, but make sure that we consolidate our learning on the grass and review as we progress.

There is no magic formula to becoming a better coach, but if we follow these principles, it will take us a long way.

Imposter syndrome

When most coaches start out, or move to a different environment, they can often suffer from 'imposter syndrome', which is a psychological pattern where individuals doubt their achievements and persistently fear being exposed as a fraud.

How you deal with imposter syndrome will depend on the individual, but for me, I have found the following steps have been helpful.

- Talking to people. If you keep your feelings to yourself, they tend to continue to build. By talking to people, it feels like a weight has been lifted from my shoulders.

- Effective and balanced reviewing. I have found that by focusing on the positives while reviewing, as well as what didn't go well, I start to feel more confident in myself in my environment.

- Accept positive feedback. I have been guilty of playing down the positive feedback that I have received in the past, but positive feedback means you are doing something well, so embrace it.

Focus on plan and review as well as do

It can be difficult to find the time to plan and review our sessions in great detail, and in the Foundation Phase, we won't plan in the same tactical detail as we would in older age groups, but having a good level of detail in our planning gives us a better chance of having a successful session.

Whether we use a pen and paper, or we plan our sessions digitally, having a good session plan will help our coaching and, in turn, help our players develop.

Reviewing sessions can have a real benefit both for ourselves and our players. Whether that is a written review, a mental review, or a review with a buddy, it will really help us recognise what we've done well and what we need to work on to help our players develop.

Get yourself a session planning resource

As mentioned, whether we use pen and paper or plan digitally, finding ourselves a session planner that fits our needs will make life easier and help us to deliver better-quality sessions.

For many years, I scribbled session plans onto a piece of paper, which worked but wasn't ideal. I ended up with folders full of different pieces of paper, but it was a nightmare when I wanted to go back through old sessions to get ideas.

Eventually, I decided to create my own PowerPoint template to plan on, which – over a few years – gave me a catalogue of sessions I could look back through.

In the last couple of years, I have changed to using a notepad to plan from, mainly because I coach full-time, and I may have two or three sessions in a day. It means I can have it to hand to refresh my mind before the session starts.

My advice would be to experiment with what works best for you.

Why review?

Session reviewing is the most underutilised aspect of the *plan-do-review* process.

If we don't review our sessions and our coaching, we are going to repeat the same mistakes.

The following quote isn't football-specific, but it's a great example of someone not learning from their experiences.

> Monty Panesar hasn't played 33 tests; he's played the same test 33 times.
>
> **Shane Warne**

Session review criteria

It's handy to have a list of areas to review. Although we don't have to go through every point, they give us points of reference.

A list also allows us to be consistent with our session reviews.

This list may seem quite daunting, and it is quite comprehensive, but we don't have to focus on every point during every session.

I came up with the following criteria to help me with my review process.

One of the biggest issues with session reviewing can be focusing too much on the negatives; it's something I've been guilty of over the years, and something I'm currently witnessing in my role as a tutor.

If things haven't gone according to plan, we need to address them (to make sure we don't repeat the same mistakes), but we should also look at what we've done well.

A great way to look at your session reviewing is to break it down into three areas.

1. What Went Well (WWW)
2. Even Better If (EBI)
3. and Things We'd Change

If you review with these areas in mind, you will focus on the positives, as well as areas of improvement.

My session review criteria

The session

- Appropriate area size
- Repetition-to-realism ratio
- Work-to-rest ratio
- Use of rules/conditions/challenges
- Managing the opposition
- Did the session support my playing and coaching philosophy?

My coaching

- Topic outcomes met
- Use and timing of coaching points

- Types of interventions used
- Clearness and positivity of communication
- Adapting the session as needed
- Linking players into units/units into the team
- Coaching position

Environment

- Fun factor
- Flow and tempo of the session
- Player ownership
- Peer-to-peer learning
- Player feedback
- Keeping the standards expected

Mistakes are learning opportunities

I have been coaching for a long time, and over the years, I've made loads of mistakes with my coaching. If I'd put on a poor session, or I felt like I'd had a negative impact on a result, it used to really get me down.

In reality, mistakes are part of life; it's what we do after making a mistake that counts. It only becomes a problem if we don't learn from our mistakes and we keep on making the same ones again and again.

We should view mistakes as learning opportunities and not beat ourselves up too much when things don't go to plan. It happens to all of us!

After a player has smashed the ball over the bar, the last thing they need is us telling them they should have got their shot on target! They know themselves!

We don't always need to correct the first mistake. If the same player continues to shoot over the bar, we can then speak to them about keeping their bodyweight further forward, or their contact point on the ball. Quite often, players will self-correct after making a mistake.

The ability to demo

Many coaches worry about the ability to demo different techniques to players, especially if they weren't the greatest players!

If someone was a former pro, or they had trials, that's great, and it will help them to demo techniques well. But, if we weren't the greatest player, and our flip flap isn't on point, don't worry.

We can practise the techniques we want to demo, and doing the demo slowed down will help players understand the technique involved. We may also find that we have players who have already got some skills and turns in their locker; there is nothing wrong with letting a player do a demo. It can actually be a really positive experience for them to be able to show what they can do to their teammates.

In all honesty, I was never the best player. I could see what I wanted to do, but my feet wouldn't always oblige! I was also an old-school full-back, who would get a nosebleed if they went over the halfway line, so 1v1 skills were very alien to me.

I've spent time over the years working on a flip flap and other skills so that I have the ability to demo them to a reasonable level, but if I have a player who can do it better than me, I will get them to demo. It means that the rest of the group sees the technique done to a good level, but it also makes the player doing the demo feel good. I tend to get the rest of the group to give them a round of applause before trying it themselves.

Catching players in, more than catching them out

On coaching courses, we get taught to see mistakes and correct them. For example, we see one of our players turning into and making contact with a defender after not scanning.

There is absolutely nothing wrong with highlighting a mistake, but make sure that we do it at the right time and don't single some players out more than others.

If we continually pull up the same player for mistakes, we can unwittingly damage that player's confidence, which in turn will lead to more mistakes.

When we can, 'catch them in', which means highlighting players doing well rather than highlighting mistakes. For example, we see a player scan then turn away from a defender.

Yes, it might not always be possible to catch players in, but when we highlight a player doing a skill, a turn, or showing good 1v1 defending technique, it can have a massively positive impact on them. Being praised by the coach in front of their teammates is really powerful.

There aren't many worse things than being singled out in front of a group of people for doing something wrong. If it's done well, then catching players out and highlighting mistakes can work, but we need to do it so players don't feel like they are being singled out.

For most kids, being made the centre of attention for something they have done well is an amazing feeling. When you can give players that feeling, why wouldn't you?

Having a technical focus over tactical

When our players get into the Youth Development Phase (YDP) and beyond, there will be plenty of time to focus on high pressing in a 1-4-3-3 or the role and responsibilities of a 4 in a 1-3-5-2. Don't be in a rush to make everything look like what we watch in the Premier League.

It's natural to see U7s swarming around the ball on match days, but the most important thing is that they learn to pass a ball, receive a ball, etc. That is not to say we can't help them keep a better shape, but don't make it our primary focus.

Players' game understanding will come over time, but a player who understands the game will struggle if they haven't worked on mastering the techniques needed to become a good player.

Length and quantity of coaching points

Foundation Phase players aren't going to have the attention span to listen to the coach talk for 5 minutes, and they won't have the mental capacity to take in loads of coaching points.

Try to keep coaching points under 30 seconds when possible. Be sharp, get in and get out. The longer we talk for, the bigger the likelihood that our players will get bored and switch off.

Think about the amount of information that we are giving. Is it going to overload players? If so, look to break it up into two or three sessions. If players are taking away two or three bits of information, we are doing a good job.

Also, remember that after sessions and games, Foundation Phase players don't need long, rambling debriefs from coaches; they tend to overload players with tons of information.

We may think, as coaches, that we have loads of great information to give to our players, but as an experienced coach once told me, "We shouldn't give all of our sweeties away at once." What he meant was that rather than talking for five minutes and giving five great coaching points, having five coaching interventions – of between 30 and 60 seconds – will have a bigger impact.

A great way to reflect on your coaching is to record yourself coaching. You don't need loads of equipment; you can buy a cheap microphone and connect it to your phone.

Listening to myself give a two-minute coaching intervention, which *should* have been at least two, if not three, separate coaching interventions, was really powerful.

Keeping a high tempo and selecting the right practices to keep players engaged

Foundation Phase players tend to be the most engaged and well-behaved when they are working hard, and sessions have a high tempo.

If we keep a high tempo during our sessions and we select the right practices – ones that have players involved all or most of the time – it will help to keep our players focused and engaged. That will make our lives easier, which certainly isn't a bad thing!

Players don't want to stand around waiting for their turn to pass, dribble, or shoot. The work-to-rest ratio is a factor, certainly, but we are better off keeping our players active and involved as much as possible.

It also links back to how quickly we can stop and then start sessions again while coaching.

The FA 4 Corner model

The FA 4 Corner Model is a holistic approach to player development that focuses on four key areas: technical/tactical, physical, psychological, and social.

So many coaches focus on the technical/tactical and physical corners, but to really improve players, coaches need to focus on all four corners.

Technical/Tactical	Psychological
Physical	Social

Coaching interventions

We may need to use command-style coaching sporadically with Foundation Phase players, but for me, focusing on Q&A and guided discovery leads to players making their own breakthroughs and having their own light bulb moments. That is more powerful than the coach telling them all of the information.

What each type of intervention means

Guided Discovery: The coach provides a player or group of players with a challenge to help them achieve the outcome. Players are encouraged to explore ways to find a solution without the coach giving them the answer. If they do not find the solution, the coach guides them towards the answer.

- **Example**. Show me how you would use your body to protect the ball.

Trial & Error: The players are provided with a challenge to solve; they are encouraged to keep going until they have solved it.

- **Example**. Try to take your first touch away from pressure.

Question & Answer: The coach leads with a question to get a response from the players. This can be used to get players to make their own breakthroughs or to check for understanding.

- **Example**. How can you stay on the ball while under pressure?

Observation & Feedback: The coach and players will observe. After observing, they will share their feedback. This will help to give players a different perspective from the outside of the practice.

- **Example**. Watch how your teammate uses their body to shield the ball from an opposition player.

Command: The coach tells or shows players how to do something. This is the most direct coaching style for giving specific instructions.

- **Example**. I want you to dribble with the ball on the safe side, away from the defender.

Joystick coaching

As a coach in the Foundation Phase, it's easy to think that telling players what to do – while they are on the ball – is helping them.

In reality, we are taking their decision-making away from them.

Coach on a match day, but leave the decisions on the ball to the players. Let them make their own mistakes and learn from them.

Joystick coaching tends to happen when the coach is worried about the result or how they are being perceived.

Observation skills

At the start of the Foundation Phase especially, most players will surround the ball. As a coach, don't get fixated on the ball.

Make sure to look around and away from the ball, as we'll probably be surprised how much we will see that we have previously missed.

In the Foundation Phase, it will look very different from what we watch on Match of the Day.

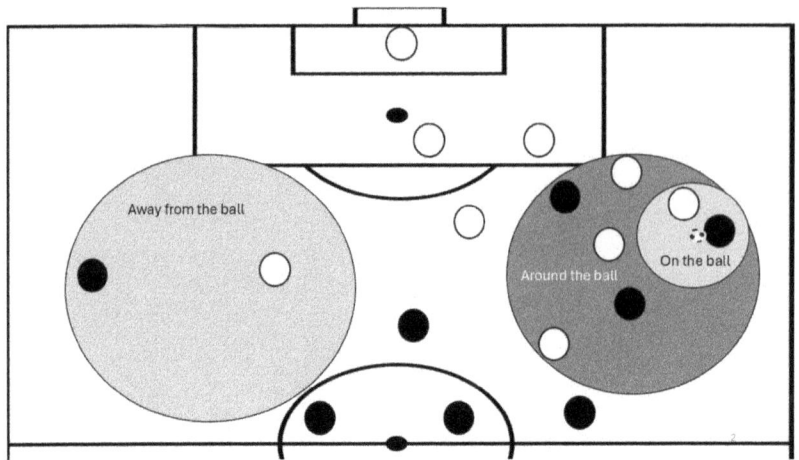

What each area means

- **On the ball:** On the ball refers to the area where the ball is when we have possession (i.e., our player in possession of the ball). It would be the opposition player with the ball when out of possession.

- **Around the ball:** Around the ball refers to the nearest players to the ball, in possession (i.e., teammates giving passing options). When out of possession, it would be players pressing and supporting the pressing player.

- **Away from the ball:** Away from the ball refers to what happens in the areas where the ball isn't. That could be on the far side of the pitch if the ball is at one side, or ahead or behind the ball, depending on which third of the pitch the ball is in.

Foundation Phase players aren't young adults!

Foundation Phase players need someone who is going to make it enjoyable above everything else.

Especially with really young kids, don't be afraid to be a little silly and larger than life with your coaching.

Foundation Phase players don't need us to be Pep or Klopp, and if that's what we want to be, we should look at coaching older players.

Creating a coaching philosophy

A coaching philosophy is a set of values, beliefs, and principles that guide a coach's approach to their work.

- **What underpins your coaching philosophy?** What matters to you as a coach? Are you driven by player development, player participation, or something else?

- **What do you want to achieve as a coach?** Do you want to become a full-time coach? Is continuous player participation a goal? Do you want to gain a UEFA A licence or help to build a club up? Write your objectives up as part of your coaching philosophy.

- **What are your values and beliefs?** What do you want your sessions and match days to look like? What are the important factors that you want to promote to your players and parents? What was important to you when you played?

- **Get your coaching philosophy written down**
Although you will be living your philosophy, it will give you something to reference.

- **Don't be afraid to tweak your philosophy.** As time goes on, we change, and what's important to us may change as well. Your philosophy should be a living document that you can update as you grow.

Roles of a Foundation Phase coach

- Coach
- Team Admin
- Team Treasurer
- Kit Person
- Physio
- Medic

- Communications Officer
- Equipment Manager
- Parent Liaison Officer
- Activity Planner
- Shoelace Tier
- Comedian

4: Practice Considerations

Football Fitness

If we only have an hour or two per week with our players, the time is best spent developing our players' ability with the ball.

We can get physical outcomes out of sessions while also getting lots of touches of the ball, which is a better way for your players to develop than laps or bleep tests.

This will change in the YDP phase, but Foundation Phase players don't need fitness training.

> A great pianist doesn't run around the piano or do push-ups with his fingers. To be great, he plays the piano. Being a footballer is not about running, push-ups, or physical work, generally. The best way to be a great footballer is to play.
>
> **Jose Mourinho**

I've seen Foundation Phase coaches doing laps, bleep tests, and hill sprints. It isn't fun for young kids, and it's not necessary.

We shouldn't be guided by what we did when we were kids — times have changed! — and we shouldn't be guided by what we see adult teams doing, as that is a completely different environment.

We can get the same physical outcomes while our players get loads of touches of the ball. Later in the book, you will find practices that get great physical corner outcomes, involve the ball, and which are also fun.

Different types of session structures

How we structure our sessions will be dependent on the age, ability, and needs of the groups we are working with. Some of the most popular ways to structure your session are...

- **Whole-part-whole.** We start with a game or more game-realistic practice, break it down to a more technical practice, and finish with something more game-realistic. We could start with a free-play game, break it down to a practice that works on your chosen topic, and then go back into a game, using a condition that gets the topic outcomes you want.

- **Technique-skill-SSG.** This is where we start off looking at the technique of the topic we are working on, then add to the realism as the session progresses. We may start with a practice that is unopposed, then into a practice that is opposed, and then into a game situation.

- **Carousel.** We divide our group and then rotate through two or more different practices. You set up practices with another coach you are working with and rotate between the different practices.

Putting together a syllabus

It's easy to be reactionary with our session planning and focus on a topic *based on the last match.*

In the longer term, we will get better results by creating or finding a syllabus that helps our group develop as players.

That could be six weeks at a time or a whole season syllabus. The main thing is that it's right for our group and our environment.

OP	IP	Transition
w/c 05/04 – 1v1 Defending (Body Shape)	n/a	n/a
w/c 12/04 – 1v1 Defending (Recap)	n/a	n/a
w/c 19/04 – n/a	n/a	Individual Movement (Before)
w/c 26/04 – n/a	Receiving (To Play Forward)	n/a
w/c 03/05 – n/a	Short Passing (Punch/Cushion)	n/a
w/c 10/05 – n/a	1v1 Attacking (Various Scenarios)	n/a

Touches, touches, touches

We want our players to be confident and comfortable on the ball, but that's hard to do if players hardly touch the ball during training sessions. If the first 20 minutes of an hour-long session is spent doing running or other fitness-based activities, that's 20

minutes that our youngsters could have spent with a ball at their feet.

The more touches a player gets, the more relaxed they will be in possession; the more times they receive the ball, the better their first touch will become.

We want our players to *want* the ball. Players who aren't comfortable with the ball at their feet are more likely to panic and kick it away. We want players who are confident to stay on the ball under pressure.

While we need to focus on getting players lots of touches in order to develop, it needs to be balanced with how much repetition versus realism they get. We will go into this next.

Balancing repetition and realism

In the Foundation Phase, we want players to get lots of repetitions of our session outcomes. It is only by repeating actions that players can gain confidence in doing them on match days.

At the same time, if players get lots of repetition but they aren't executing what they are learning in more complex, game-like situations, they will struggle on match days when they suddenly have lots of decisions to make with teammates and opposition players around them.

Finding the correct balance between repetition and realism may change from session to session depending on the topic, but finding a good balance will help players learn and fulfil their potential.

Practise choice to balance repetition and realism

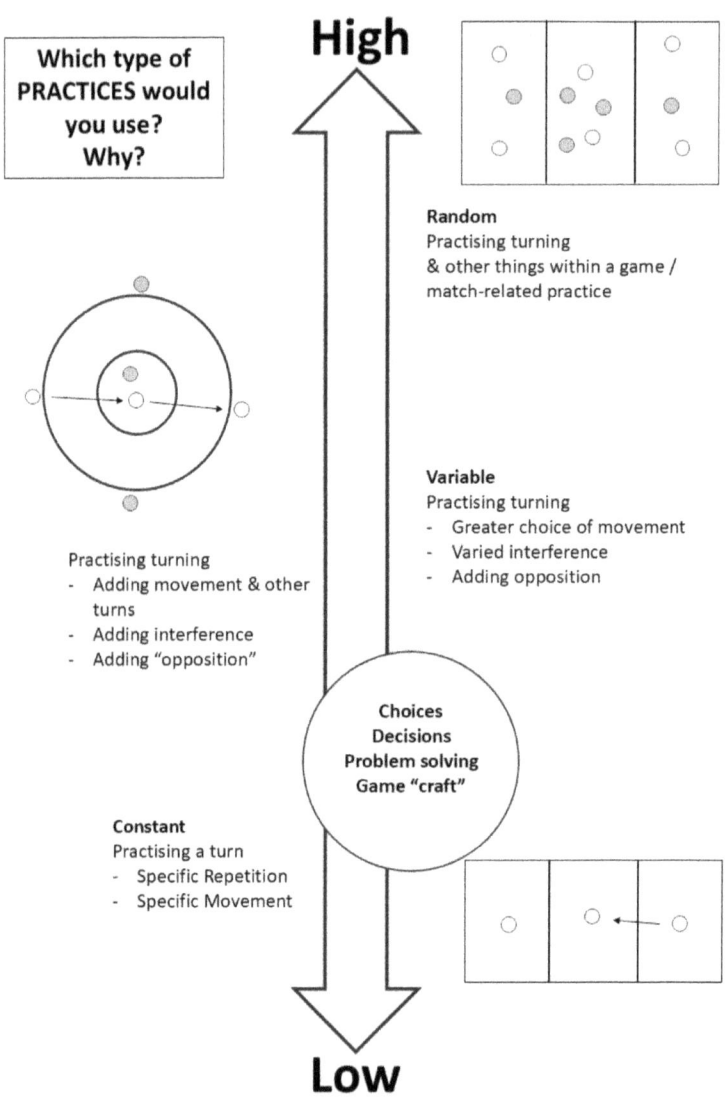

Looking to balance repetition and realism with my sessions was a massive lightbulb moment for me. How that balance will look will be different for every group and will depend on a number of factors, including age, ability level, understanding of the topic, etc.

If it is a new topic or a topic that the players don't have much experience of, you will want to use practices that are more towards the constant end of the spectrum (see the next section), but don't forget that match time is important as well.

Constant practices

Constant practices involve players repeating specific techniques to develop them or refine them. Some examples of constant practices would be unopposed versions of…

- Ball mastery

- Passing practices

- Finishing practices

- Receiving to turn and play forward

- Dribbling and running with the ball practices

Variable practices

Variable practices involve players practising a skill in a variety of different situations under varying conditions and levels of pressure. Examples of variable practices would be…

- Ball mastery with defenders added

- Rondos

- Possession practices

- Finishing practices with defenders
- Wave practices

Random practices

Random practices are practices that resemble the game, where players get the chance to practise skills in game-realistic situations. Examples of random practices would be…

- Small-sided games (SSG's)
- Conditioned games
- Phases of play

Transitions between practices

Our transitions between practices are more important than we might think. Foundation Phase players don't have the longest attention spans, and if we spend ages moving cones around or explaining practices, we are likely to lose them.

When explaining practices, a whiteboard is a great help, as well as having the practice set out so that they can see it. If we can set the bibs up in the areas/positions we want our players in, it also gives them a valuable visual aid.

Transitioning between practices is easier when we have a lot of space, and when we can move between them quickly and easily. If we have limited space, it becomes harder. Sharing our session plans with a buddy coach (so they can move cones while we explain the session) or planning our sessions so that we are using similar setups throughout will help transition between practices quickly.

Players will tend to lose interest if they are stood around, which will happen if you need five minutes to set up the next practice.

The best sessions are the ones where players are almost constantly moving, apart from coaching points and drinks breaks.

Ball rolling time

Ball rolling time in the Foundation Phase should be a high priority. The English FA says that we should aim towards 70% ball rolling time, but in the Foundation Phase, the aim should be nearer 80%, when possible. Naturally, this will be dependent on things like topic, space, drink breaks, etc.

The main things to avoid are things like line drills, where lots of players are waiting for turns, and long coaching points, where players are standing around. Young players don't have a particularly long attention span, so remember to make your coaching points simple and quick.

A high ball rolling time will also result in better physical outcomes for our players; the more active they are, the harder they work.

For me, a great way of judging a good Foundation Phase session is when the players are surprised that it has already finished when the session ends!

When you hear "We've finished already?" from players, it tends to mean that time has flown by, usually because you've kept them engaged, kept a high ball rolling time, and transitioned between practices quickly.

Another good indicator is when players ask to carry on for a few more minutes at the end of the session. If they want to carry on playing, rather than running to their car, it means you are doing something right.

Avoiding line drills

A line drill is a practice where a group of players wait in line while one or two players take their turn at an activity. They are usually used for finishing practices, as well as 1v1 attacking and defending practices. They take valuable touches and ball rolling time away from players and can be avoided by using practices that keep players moving or which have very little waiting time.

You can have a 1v1 or 2v2 wave practice (replicating a continuous flow of play) where some players are waiting, but players shouldn't be waiting two or three minutes for a turn. If you have a bigger group, you can split the group up and have two of the same practices side by side, with a coach running each practice, to avoid players waiting for too long.

Session timings

It's good to have timings in mind for each of your practices, as it will help you to deliver structured sessions. But you shouldn't be too rigid with your timings.

If you have planned to deliver a practice for 15 minutes, and it is going amazingly well, with the players enjoying themselves and the practice delivering the outcomes you want, why cut it off to go onto another practice? If it means that you run the practice for an extra five or ten minutes and cut another practice short, that isn't an issue.

On the flip side, if a practice isn't working, look to adapt it in real time so that it does work. After that, though, don't feel like you need to persevere with it if the players don't understand it or it does not work with your group. Go on to the next practice or into a game, then reflect – after the session – on why it did not work.

Managing difference

The vast majority of grassroots teams will have players with a mix of different abilities, and this can be a challenge for coaches. Trying to make sure that the players who are excelling continue to be challenged, while the players who need extra help receive support, can be made a lot easier by getting to know your players and understanding their individual needs, then using the S.T.E.P. principles (below) to adapt sessions to help all your players develop.

If you work as a coaching pair (more on that coming up), splitting practices makes sense, so we work with different parts of the group based on their needs. Likewise, pairing and grouping players based on ability – at various points during a session – is another good way to manage differences.

S.T.E.P. principle

The S.T.E.P. principle stands for Space, Task, Equipment, and People. Coaches use it to adapt practices to ensure they work for their group of players, allowing for different levels of challenge and support.

- **Space:** Refers to the environment and how it affects the practice. Coaches can modify the size of the playing area, distance, or the number of participants in the space.

- **Task:** Focuses on the rules, objectives, and the structure of the practice. It could be adapted by changing the number of passes required, the scoring method, or the use of specific skills.

- **Equipment:** Includes the tools and resources used in the practice. Changes can involve the size or type of equipment, or the use of different types of balls.

- **People:** Considers the players involved in the practice, including their abilities and needs. This involves adapting the practice to suit specific players or groups, making sure to manage differences inside the groups and supporting the needs of players.

Don't be afraid to make things messy!

We may think that if practices appear really organised – with lots of cones and neat lines – it will look impressive and make us look good to other coaches and parents. That may be true to a certain extent, but it may be doing a disservice to our players. By making things messy and adding an element of chaos, we can really benefit our players to develop things like decision-making and scanning skills.

Rather than having lots of 1v1s in neat boxes, why not have them all in the same area? That way, players are getting repetitions of 1v1s but with a level of interference from other pairs.

When playing a game, why not add a second ball at points? Yes, it takes away from game realism, but it adds more decisions, communication, scanning and touches.

Remember, if practices look chaotic, they may well be giving better outcomes over practices in neat lines with loads of cones.

I always used to worry about what other coaches or parents watching from the sidelines thought about my sessions.

If there were neat lines and players looking like they were organised, I thought that people would think I knew what I was doing, and I was doing a good job.

It was only once I realised that my players' development was more important than what people watching the session thought, that I put development first and aesthetics second.

The importance of playing matches during training sessions

Every youngster wants to play a match. I'm sure we've all been asked, 'When are we having a match?' at many of our training sessions! Although it's got to be balanced with repetition, the best way to help players develop and experience the game is by *playing the game*.

Playing a match at the end of training shouldn't just be used as a carrot to get good behaviour from your players. And it shouldn't be something we do for the last 10 minutes of sessions if players have behaved well.

Whether it's free-play or we add a condition to our game, players enjoy matches. They give the highest amount of realism away from a match day.

Coaching as a pair

A buddy coach is a second coach we are working with. If we are without a second coach for any reason, we can often use a parent to help us.

- We could use our buddy coach to serve balls to keep the tempo high.

- We could get our buddy coach to work with individuals while we work on the whole group.

- In small-sided games, we could work with one team while our buddy coach works with the other.

- To keep the ball rolling time high, one of us could set the next practice up while the other manages the practice currently being delivered.

We shouldn't be tempted to use our buddy coach as an extra player to make up numbers – it takes touches away from players, as well as being a potential health and safety risk.

Having a good working relationship with the coach we collaborate with makes everything much easier for both of us. When planning sessions, we can either plan parts of the session each (so that we both deliver) or take turns planning the whole session. That way, if a practice is going well, we don't feel the need to stop it and move to the next practice, as the other coach has planned it.

When working as a pair and coaching inside the session, for me, the best way to maximise your impact is to have a group coach and an individuals coach. The group coach focuses (as the name suggests) on group practices, timings, and coaching points. The individual coach focuses on individual players to help them with particular technical outcomes from the session.

Working with goalkeepers

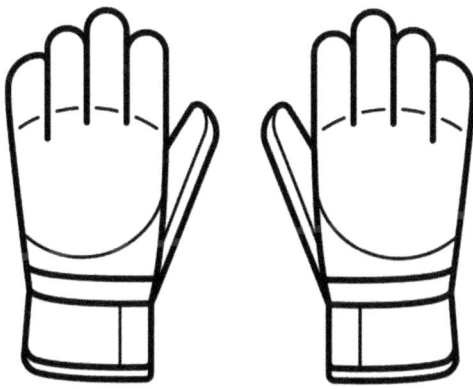

Really, we should rotate around our players so that everyone gets to experience being in goal, *especially* early in the Foundation Phase. We may have one or two players who either seem to be more advanced than the others or who just really want to be a goalkeeper.

By making them a full-time goalkeeper early on, and having them focus on goalkeeping while the rest of the team is working with the ball at their feet, it may potentially help them in the short term, but they are missing out on lots of valuable touches with their feet.

The modern goalkeeper has roughly 70% of their touches with their feet and 30% with their hands, so touches are valuable, as is involving goalkeepers in outfield practices.

It could well be that your best outfield player is your best goalkeeper. Some of the world's best keepers didn't specialise until the YDP phase, players like Joe Hart and David Ge Gea, for example.

In the same way that we work with outfield players, we should also focus on our goalkeepers' ability to play off both feet. This will help them to receive and distribute the ball.

Finding practices

There are a variety of different places to find practices, including in the next chapter. We can buy books of session plans and find them online, in coaching magazines, on courses, or at CPD events.

Social media is another excellent place to find practices, with the @SundayShare10 on X (formally known as Twitter) being a great place to find ideas.

When we find sessions, context is king. A Man City pressing phase of play may look great, but it probably won't work with a Foundation Phase group. When we find a practice, we should view it through the lens of our group, and ask ourselves if it will work without having to adapt it or how we can adapt it to work with our group.

Not every session needs all new practices

While it's exciting to find new practices and use them with your group, it is worth putting together a selection of practices which you know deliver the outcomes you want, as well as ones that are player favourites.

Archiving favourite practices can make planning easier if you are short on time, as you can refer back to them. Having a store of practices also helps you when you are coaching and you need to adapt to different numbers or when the practice you are using is not working.

5: Practices

How to view these practices

I have selected a few of my Foundation Phase favourite practices from my years working in this area. With a few exceptions, they should work with any group, although some adaptation may be required. Accordingly, consider ages, abilities, and the number of players you are coaching.

Not every session needs 'all-new' practices; put together a selection of practices that work for you.

While it's exciting to find new practices and use them with your group, it is worth putting together a selection of practices as you go.

- Collect practices which you know will deliver the outcomes you want.

- Have go-to practices that are player favourites.

- Collecting favourite practices can make planning easier if you are short on time (as you can refer back to them quickly).

- Favourite practices are useful when you need to adapt to different numbers or when your practice is not working.

Ball Mastery

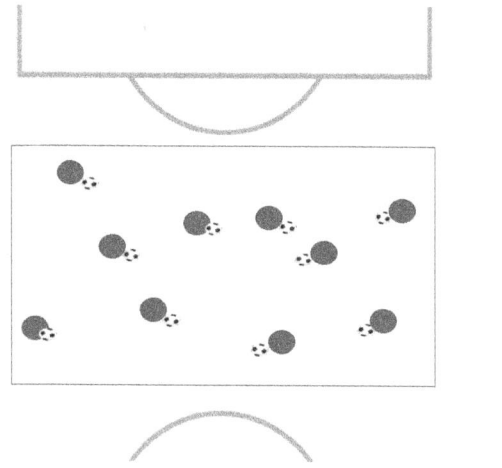

Description

Ball mastery is a key tool for developing players' techniques on the ball, while also helping them become comfortable in possession of the ball by giving them lots of touches.

Set up

Set up a space to suit your number of players and their abilities, with a ball per player.

Focus on different techniques with the ball, like dribbling, running with the ball, and 1v1 skills and turns, while players move around the area.

Topics the practice covers

1v1 skills

Scanning

Ball control

Turning

Dribbling

Progressions

Make the area smaller to add more interference from players moving around.

Add a defender who looks to win balls off players, then either keeps possession until the player who lost possession wins it back, or who scores in a goal after winning the ball.

Traffic Lights

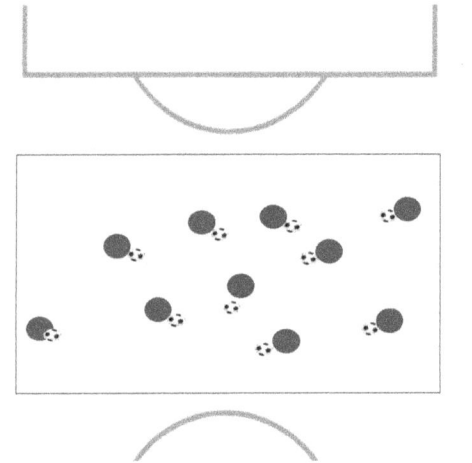

Description

Traffic Lights is a ball mastery variation that helps players to scan while moving with the ball, as they need to scan while they are moving with the ball to see which cone the coach is holding up.

Set up

Set up a space to suit your players' ability, with a ball per player.

The coach holds up one of three cones while the players move around the area with the ball.

To start with, green means run with the ball, yellow means dribble, and red means stop.

Topics the practice covers

Dribbling

Running with the ball

1v1 skills

Turns

Scanning

Progressions

Change the meaning of one or more cones to a 1v1 skill or a turn, deceleration or acceleration, or anything else you want to work on.

King of the Ring

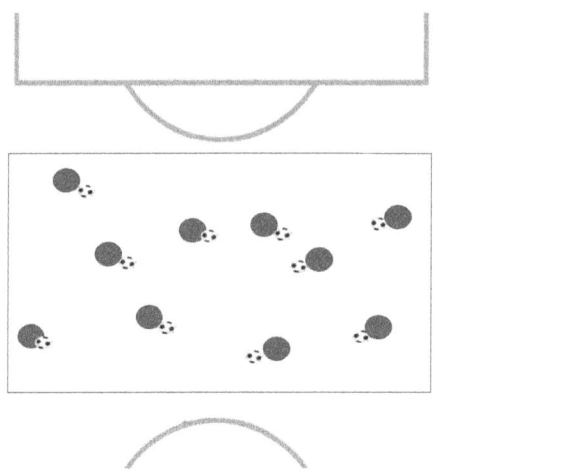

Description

King of the Ring is a great practice to help players retain possession of the ball, but – in its original form – it leads to a lot of players standing around, so I have modified it.

Set up

Set up the space to suit your players' ability and give every player a ball each.

When the game starts, players get a point every time they kick another player's ball out of the area.

If a player's ball gets kicked out, they retrieve it and carry on playing.

The player with the most points at the end of each round wins.

Players can only kick a ball out if their ball is close to them.

Topics the practice covers

1v1 skills

Scanning

Ball control

Turning

Dribbling

Progressions

If you have a very mixed-ability group, you can set up two or more games to make the challenge right for individuals.

Gates Game

Description

Gates games are a great way to work on dribbling, with lots of ways to adapt the practice, allowing players to work on dribbling and running with the ball.

Set up

Set up cone gates in your area, use different colours, and have a scoring system, so some coloured cone gates are worth more than others.

Players have a ball each, and they play two-minute rounds. For each round, players look to dribble through as many gates as possible. At the end, they count up their points and aim to beat that number in the next round.

Topics the practice covers

1v1 skills

Dribbling

Running with the ball

Scanning

Turning

Progressions

Rather than dribbling through a gate, players perform a 1v1 skill while dribbling through, or use a type of turn before dribbling away from the gate to score a point.

Add two or three defenders into the gates. If players can dribble through a gate with a defender, it's worth ten points.

The Stadium Game

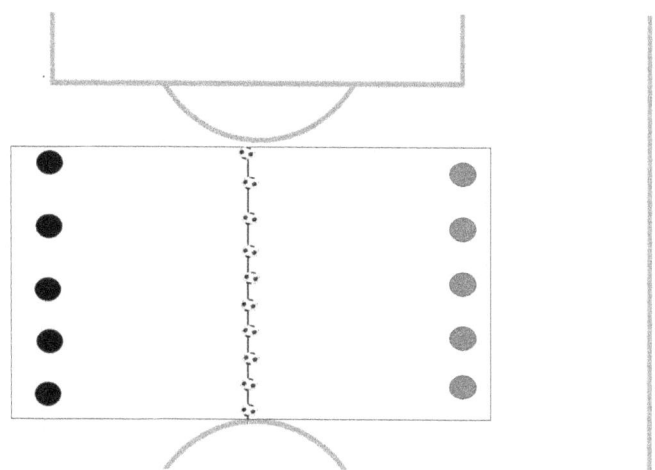

Description

The Stadium Game is a practice with lots of different outcomes, both in and out of possession, with each team trying to get more footballs in their half than the opposition.

Set up

Split the group into two teams. Each team has half the area (their zone), and balls are set up to divide the two areas.

When the coach says go, both teams have to get the footballs and take them into their half.

To start with, players are only trying to steal; they can't tackle opposition players.

Topics the practice covers

Dribbling

Running with the ball

1v1 skills

1v1 defending

Shielding

Progressions

Players can try to tackle opposition players while they try to steal balls.

Rather than everyone looking to steal footballs, teams can have some players defend the footballs in their half, while others look to steal footballs from the opposition half.

Skills Corridor

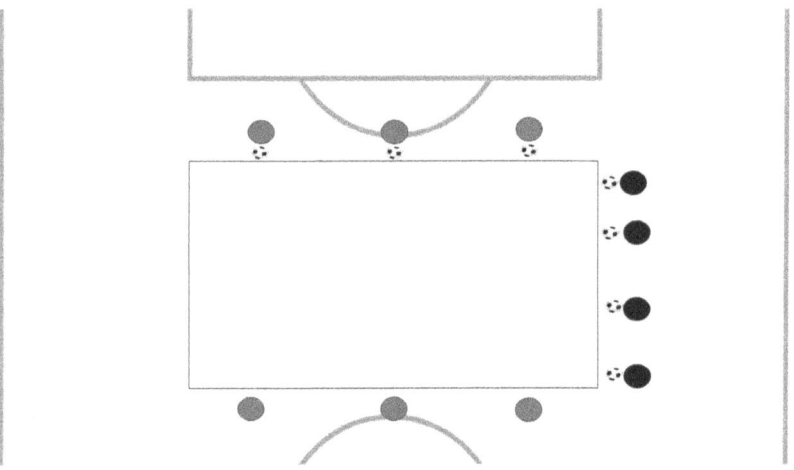

Description

Skills Corridor is a practice that can be adapted to fit your squad's needs and gets lots of in possession outcomes. In this form, the players in the central corridor dribble through, while the pairs on the outside pass between each other.

Set up

Set your area up with a central corridor, and outside zones for the passing players.

The players in the corridor look to dribble from one end to the other, either turning at the end to go back through, or going around the outside of the practice and back to the start.

You can get players to practise skills while they go through the corridor, and different turns at the ends.

The passing players in pairs look to pass to each other through the area without the ball hitting a dribbling player.

Topics the practice covers

Dribbling

Running with the ball

1v1 skills

Turns

Passing

Scanning

Progressions

If it is too difficult for your players in this form, you can start without the passing players. Instead, you can put cones in the central area they have to dribble around.

Swap the passing and dribbling players so they get to practise both outcomes.

Tag Games

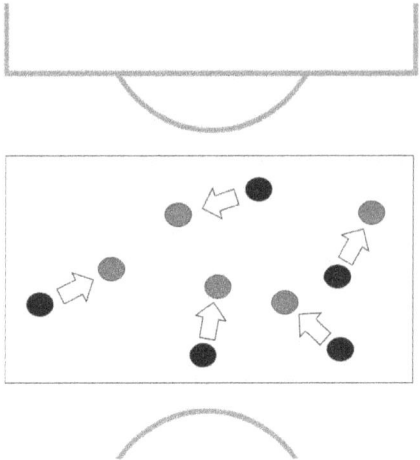

Description

Tag games are a great way to work on ABCS and get lots of physical outcomes while also being lots of fun. When you include balls, you get lots of technical outcomes as well as touches on the ball.

Set up

The most basic tag game is two-team tag, where one team is taggers, and the other team look to avoid being tagged.

Both teams have a turn as taggers and avoiders.

At the end of the game, the team with the most tags wins.

Topics the practice covers

Agility

Balance

Coordination

Speed

Scanning

Dribbling

Turning

Progressions

Add balls in, so the players avoiding being tagged do it while dribbling, and the taggers can only tag while in control of their ball.

There are lots of other fun tag games that you can use.

Chicken or Hero

Description

Chicken or Hero is a player favourite, and it's a lot like Bulldog. Without a ball, it works on players' ABCS; with a ball, it works on dribbling, running with the ball, and 1v1 skills to beat a player.

Set up

You start with one tagger in the middle who calls a player's name; the chosen player has to either shout out "chicken" or "hero".

If they shout chicken, everybody tries to run to the other end without being tagged.

If they shout hero, they try to run to the other end on their own without being tagged. Everyone else runs after the player who shouted hero until they are tagged or have made it to the other end.

The last player to be tagged wins.

Topics the practice covers

Agility

Balance

Coordination

Speed

Recognising when to exploit space

Dribbling

Running with the ball

1v1 skills

Progressions

Make the space smaller to make it more challenging for the non-taggers to get across the area.

Add balls in for the non-taggers. The tagger must win their ball and score in a goal or mini goal to turn the player who lost the ball into a tagger. If a non-tagger loses their ball, they can win it back before a tagger scores.

1v1 Tournament

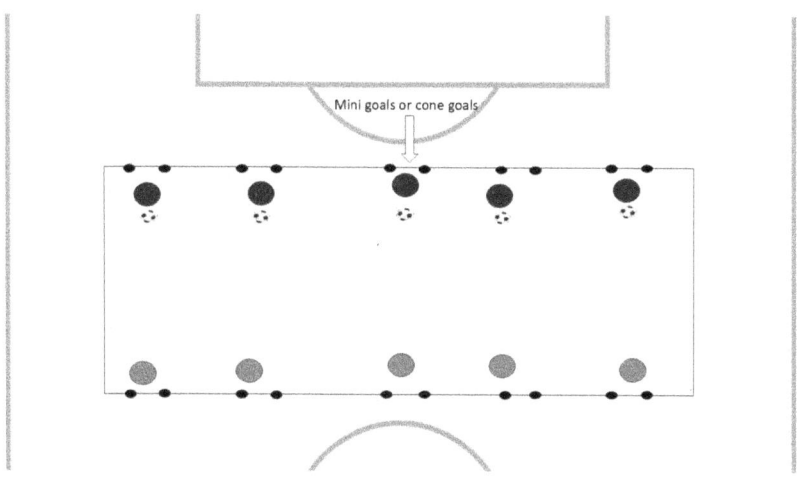

Description

A 1v1 tournament is a great way to work on attacking or defending 1v1. It is a very competitive practice that players enjoy.

Set up

Set up pitches for the number of players you have, the top pitch being the Premier League, the next pitch being the Championship, etc.

Put players into 1v1 games.

To score a point, players dribble through the opponent's gate.

At the end of each game, the winner goes up a pitch, and the loser goes down. If it is a draw, they rock, paper, scissors to see who goes up and who goes down.

Topics the practice covers

1v1 skills

1v1 defending

Body feints

Turns

Progressions

If you have odd numbers, you can either have a Premier League winner, who has a one-minute challenge while a game is going on (keep ups, a skill, turn, etc.), or you can make one game a 2v1 (which can be used to help a player who is struggling, or challenge a player who is forging ahead).

Turn it into a 2v2 tournament to work on paired attacking and defending.

1v1 to Stay on the Ball

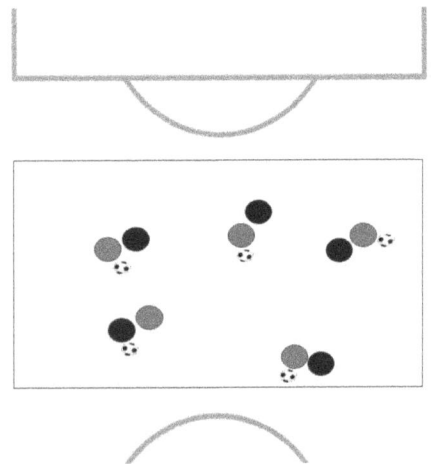

Description

Many coaches only practice 1v1s when the attacker and defender are fronted up against each other.

However, 1v1s happen in lots of different situations, and this practice is great for working on in and out of possession. It develops players' ability to stay on the ball by using 1v1 skills, turns, and shielding the ball. Out of possession, it works on how players can win the ball in different situations through tackling and using body and limbs to separate the player in possession from the ball.

Set up

Set players up in pairs, with a ball per pair. They rock, paper, scissors to see who starts.

Play one-minute rounds; the player in the pair who has possession of the ball at the end of the round wins.

If the ball goes out of the area, the player who did not have possession can dribble on.

Topics the practice covers

1v1 skills

1v1 defending

Turns

Shielding

Body and limbs

Progressions

If everyone working in one area is too challenging, split the area into separate 1v1 pitches.

Turn it into 2v2s to stay on the ball in pairs.

Rondos

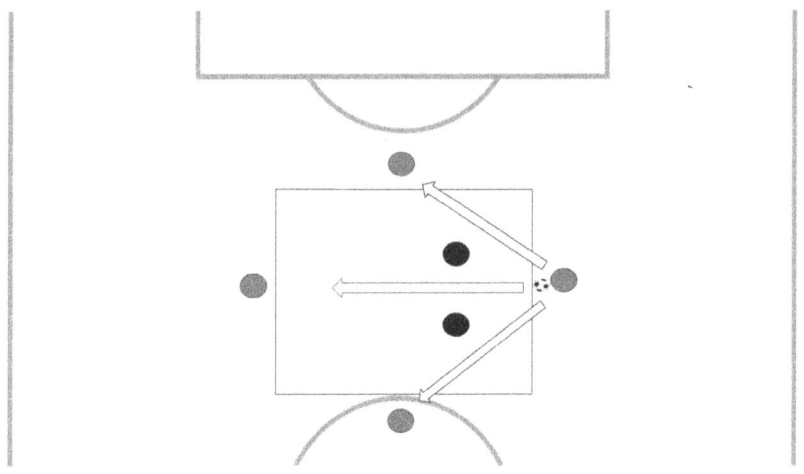

Description

What probably springs to mind when you read the word rondo is a large circular rondo with lots of players on the outside, but there are loads of variations. Here, we have a 4v2 rondo. Rondos are a great way to get many in or out of possession outcomes. In possession, players are working on passing and receiving. Out of possession, players are working on pressing, covering, tackling and intercepting.

Set up

The four players on the outside look to keep possession of the ball by passing between each other and keeping the ball away from the two defenders.

If the defenders win the ball by intercepting a pass or tackling the player in possession, they switch with the players who lost the ball and the player to their left.

Topics the practice covers

Passing

Receiving

Movement

Pressing

Covering

Progressions

Think about your players when deciding on your rondo. With younger players, you may want to adapt it into a 4v1 and use a bigger area to help the players in possession gain more success. With older age groups, you could look at other variations, like 3v1 rondos or two-zone rondos.

The Zoo Game

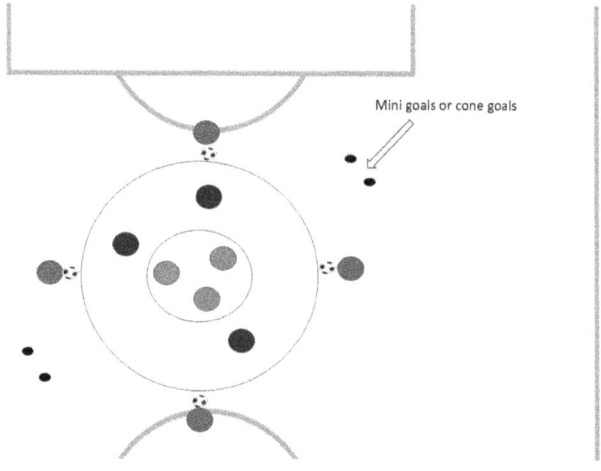

Description

This is a practice I picked up many years ago from the FA Youth Module 1. It is a great example of adding a story to a practice when working with younger players to spark their imagination.

Set up

Set your space up with an inner and outer circle.

The outside players are the visitors, the players inside the outer circle are zookeepers, and the players in the middle circle are the zoo animals.

The visitors get a point every time they play into an animal without the zookeepers intercepting the ball, and the animals get a point every time they pass the ball back to the visitors.

The zookeepers get a point by intercepting the ball and breaking out to score in a mini goal. When they break out, the visitors can try to stop them from scoring.

Topics the practice covers

Passing

Receiving

Breaking lines

Intercepting

Teamwork

Progressions

Switch the players around so that they can experience each role.

Change the balance of players in each area if they find it too easy or difficult.

The Transfer Game

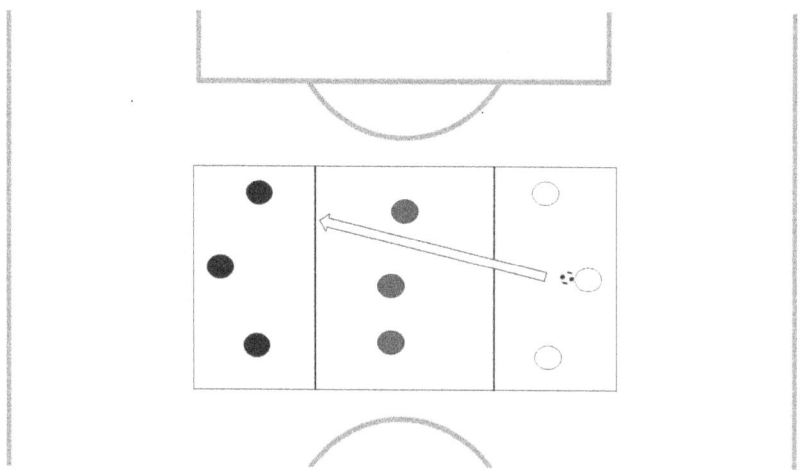

Description

The Transfer Game is my favourite practice because it has loads of great outcomes for different coaching topics and lots of different ways to adapt it. In possession, it works on keeping possession and breaking lines. Out of possession, it works on pressing, cover, and balance.

Set up

Set your players up into three teams in a third each. The teams in the outside thirds look to keep possession between them.

The team in the middle third can have a player go into an outside third to press, while the players in the middle look to intercept passes.

The team in the middle get a point every time they win or intercept the ball.

When the team in the middle wins the ball, they play it to the other outside team.

Switch teams around so each team has a turn in the middle.

Topics the practice covers

Passing

Receiving

Scanning

Pressing

Covering

Progressions

Place goals behind the outside thirds. When the team in the middle wins the ball, they look to score in the goal of the team that lost it.

Rather than getting a point every time you win the ball, the team that wins the ball switches places with the team that lost the ball, and the team that lost the ball goes into the middle.

Robin Hood

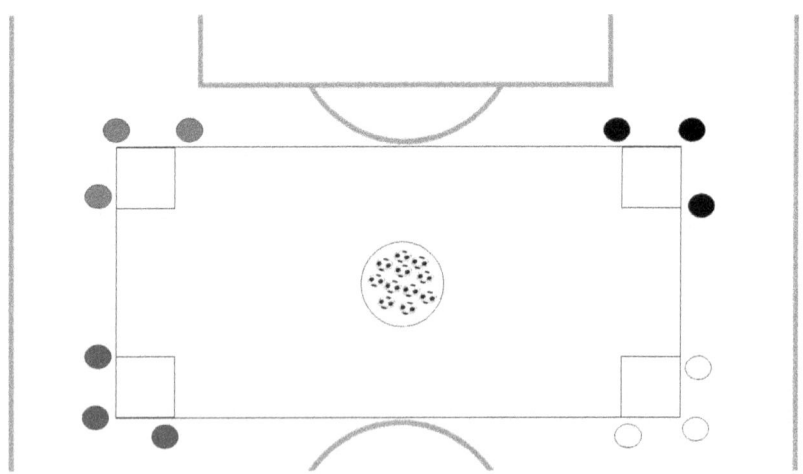

Description

Robin Hood is a classic from the old Level 1 when I started coaching. It's still a player favourite which gets very competitive!

Set up

Split your group into four teams.

Set up a zone in each corner for teams to place the footballs they've collected, and a central area where the balls start.

When the coach says go, teams look to collect balls from the central area by running out one at a time, collecting a football, then dribbling it back to their zone and tagging a teammate to go.

Once all of the balls have been collected from the centre, teams can start taking balls from other teams' corners.

At the end of three minutes, the team with the most footballs in their corner wins.

Topics the practice covers

Dribbling

Running with the ball

Teamwork

Communication

Shielding

Progressions

Let the players who aren't taking a football from an opposition corner try to shield their footballs.

Battleships

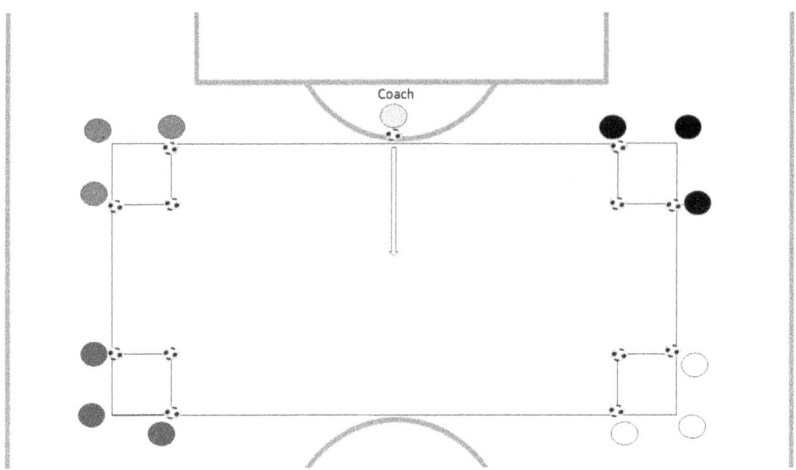

Description

Battleships is a fun game that gets very competitive and has many outcomes throughout the four corners.

Set up

Split your group into four teams, and number the players in each team (one to three on each team in this example).

Have three footballs on cones in each corner.

The coach calls a number and serves a ball in.

The players who are that number on each team run in and try to knock a ball off another team's cones with the ball that is in play.

Topics the practice covers

Dribbling

Running with the ball

Ball striking

Teamwork

Communication

Progressions

Call more than one number so two or more players from each team go in.

Let teams 'team up' and work together with another team once they have lost all of their footballs.

Possession v Pressure

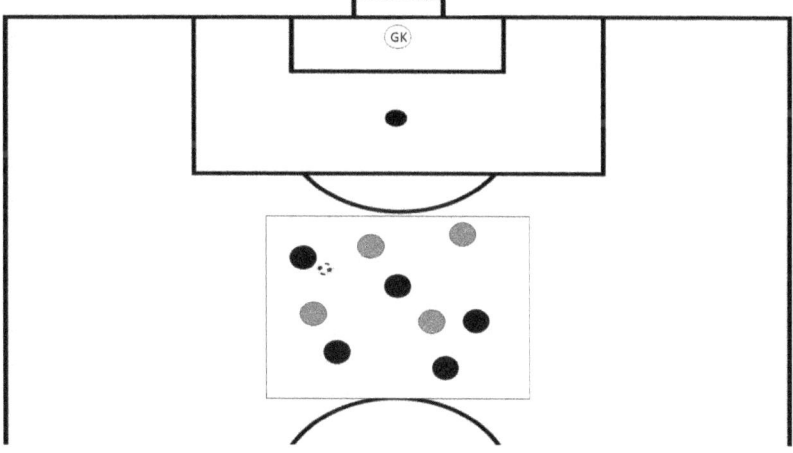

Description

This practice works better with the older age groups in the Foundation Phase, with many in possession and out of possession outcomes. One team looks to score points by completing a set number of passes; the other team looks to win the ball and then break out to score.

Set up

Set up an area to suit the ability of your players, with a goal to break out to, outside the area.

Give the possession team an overload to help them keep possession. If they keep the ball, they get a point after a set number of passes. The pressing team look to win the ball.

Once a pressing player has won possession, they break out and the coach serves another ball into the possession team while the pressing player who has won the ball goes to shoot.

Topics the practice covers

Pass detail

Movement

Playing forward

Pressing

Finishing

Progressions

Change the balance between possession and pressing players if it is too easy for either team.

Allow a defending player to break out to win the ball back once the pressing player who has won the ball has broken out.

Have a defending player outside the box to help the goalkeeper.

Allow two players to break out and combine to score.

Numbers Game

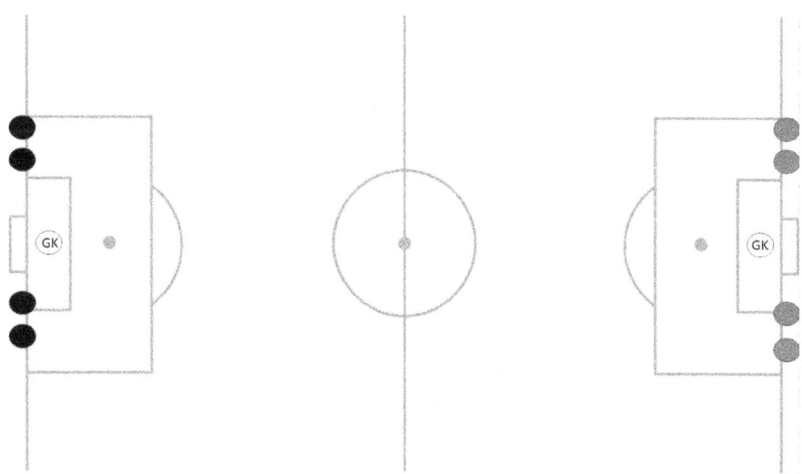

Description

The Numbers Game is a great practice for attacking and defending, with the flexibility to have equal numbers or overloads and underloads.

Set up

Players are split into two teams, with a goalkeeper on each team.

The outfield players on each team are given a number.

The coach serves the ball in and shouts out a number. The players on each team whose numbers have been called look to score in the opponent's goal.

Topics the practice covers

1v1 skills

1v1 defending

Attacking and defending with overloads and underloads

Passing

Finishing

Progressions

Call out two or more numbers from each team.

Call out more numbers from one team and fewer from another (Example - Orange team numbers 1, 2, 3; Blue team numbers 1, 2 to create overloads and underloads.

Gladiators

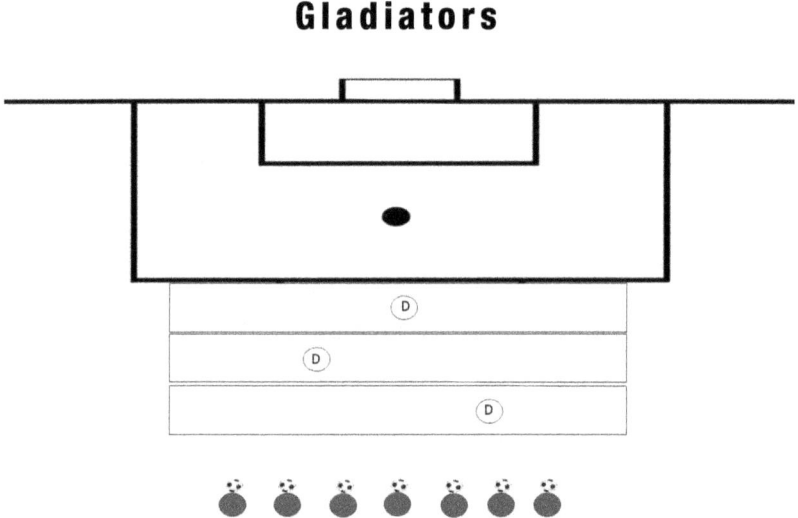

Description

Gladiators is a fun practice that works on players' decision-making on when to dribble or run with the ball, while also looking at finishing.

Set up

Set the area up with a goal at one end, and three coned areas for the defenders, as well as mini goals for the defenders to score in when they win the ball.

All the attackers can go at the same time. Here, we are helping them to understand when to dribble or run with the ball, depending on whether there is a defender in front of them or not.

The attackers have to progress through the defenders' areas, and score a goal. If they make it through and score, they go around the outside of the practice and start again.

If the defenders tackle attackers, they score by passing the ball into the mini goals, then the attacker who lost their ball starts again. Play for two- or three-minute rounds.

Topics the practice covers

Dribbling

Running with the ball

1v1 skills

1v1 defending

Shooting

Progressions

Switch roles so everyone gets a go at being attackers and defenders.

Add or take away defenders if the group is finding it too difficult or too easy.

Finishing Wave Practice

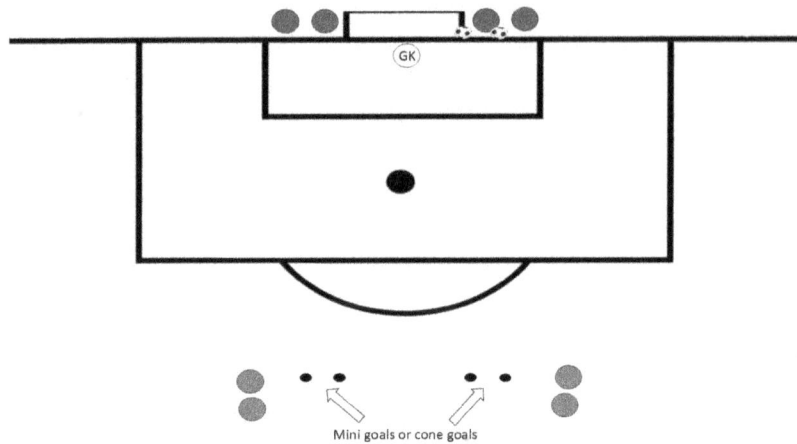

Description

All players love a finishing practice! Here, we have a 2v2 to finish practice, but there are lots of different variations you can use.

With younger players, you may start with an unopposed finishing practice and then build up from there. With this practice, you can focus on attacking as individuals or pairs to finish inside the box when in possession. You can also focus on defending as individuals or pairs in and around the box when out of possession.

Set up

Set up using realistic pitch markings, if possible.

Have a goalkeeper in the main goal, and mini goals or cone goals for the defenders to score into if they win the ball.

The defenders dribble out halfway towards the attackers, then pass the ball to them so that the defenders start in a game-realistic position.

The attackers try to score, while the defenders look to win the ball and score in the mini goals or cone goals.

After each turn, the defenders go to the attacking stations, and the attackers go to the defending stations.

Topics the practice covers

Shooting

1v1 skills

2v2 attacking

1v1 defending

2v2 defending

Passing

Turns

Progressions

You can start unopposed and build it up to a 1v1 before going to 2v2.

You can also adapt the practice to have attacking overloads to help the attackers gain success.

Three-Team Finishing

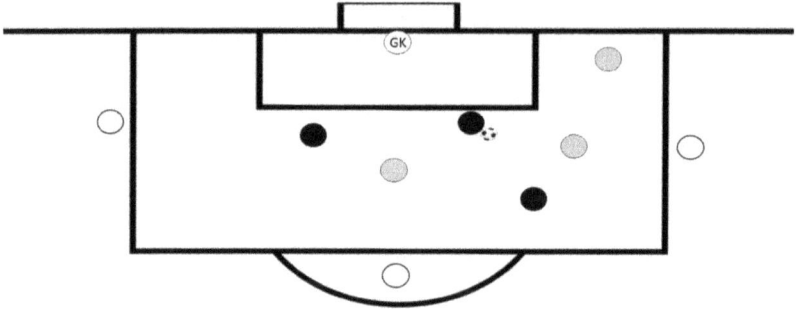

Description

This is a great practice for working on finishing outcomes in a game-realistic practice.

Set up

Use a penalty box for the area with a goal. Split the group into three teams, with a goalkeeper.

When a team has the ball, they need to make three passes between themselves and the outside players before they can score.

If the defending team inside the box wins the ball, they have to play out to the outside players before becoming the attacking team and making three passes before scoring.

If the goalkeeper gets the ball, he plays with the team that is defending to pass the ball to the outside players.

Topics the practice covers

Passing

Movement

Shooting

1v1 skills

1v1 defending

Teamwork

Progressions

Switch roles, so each group has a go at being the outside players.

Take off the pass limit, so the team in possession can score as soon as they have combined with an outside player.

Conditioned and other SSGs

Two Different Balls game

Each team can only score with *their* ball; they must look to defend against the other team's ball.

Multi-Ball game

Add a second or third ball to the SSG at different points in the game, so two or three balls are in play.

Back-to-Back Goal game

Place the goals back-to-back in the middle of the pitch.

Football Ice Hockey

The goals are brought forward, with space behind so that players can play around the back of them.

Football Rugby

Players can't pass forward, only sideways or backwards.

Football Basketball

A shot has to be taken before the shot clock goes off.

More Passes = More Points

The number of passes a team makes before scoring is how much their goal is worth.

You Can Only Win By 1 Goal

Once you score, you need to keep possession and stop the opposition from scoring.

Score Within 6 Seconds of Winning Possession = Triple Goals

This game encourages pressing and positivity after transitions.

Goals Scored after Winning the Ball in the Opposition Half = Triple Goals

Press high to win possession.

Maximum of 5 Passes Before Shooting

Look to be positive and direct in possession.

1 Touch or 4+ Touches Only

Think about when to play quickly or stay on the ball/exploit space. Players need to scan to recognise what is around them and make correct decisions.

Goals from Crosses = 3 Goals

Work on creating crossing situations, and attacking crosses.

Secret Scorer

Teams choose a player on their team whose goals are worth three.

Secret Scorer and Assister

Teams choose a player on their team whose goals are worth three, and an assister whose assists are worth three.

World Cup Final Scenario

One team starts 2-0 up but have had a player sent off. They have five minutes to hold on for the win, underloaded. The opposition look to get back into the game with an overload.

Bielsa Murder Ball / Non-stop Football

No corners, throw-ins, etc. When the ball goes out, another one is played straight in to keep a high ball rolling time.

The Dice Game

When a player scores, they roll the dice. 1, 2, and 3 are a positive outcome like double goals, the goal counts and you get a penalty, etc. 4, 5 and 6 are a negative outcome, like the goal does not count, the goal counts but the opposition have a penalty, etc.

Messi Bib

Give one player the Messi bib. That player is not allowed to pass; they can only beat players and shoot.

Finishing Noughts and Crosses

Played as a normal game. When a player scores, they mark on the board what their team scored with (use magnets, small flat markers or a pen). The first team to get three different finishes in a row wins (e.g., volley, side foot, laces).

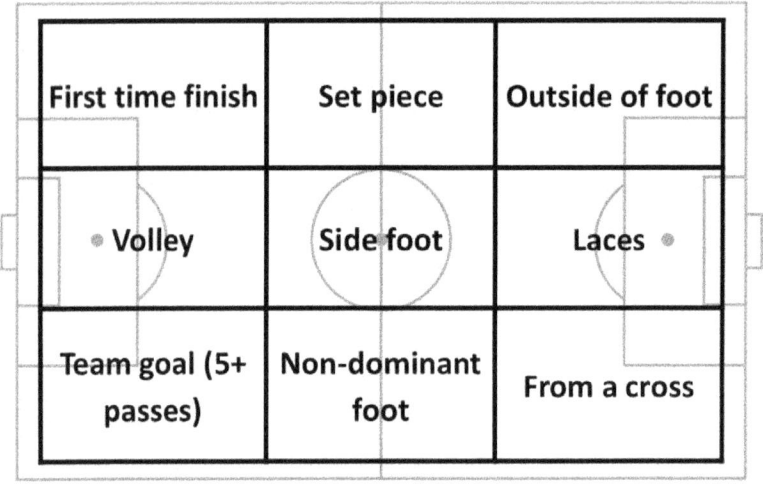

First time finish	Set piece	Outside of foot
Volley	Side foot	Laces
Team goal (5+ passes)	Non-dominant foot	From a cross

6: Technical Detail

Technical Detail underpins everything in football. Beneath formations and styles of play are the techniques that players need to learn to be successful on the pitch. In the Foundation Phase, focusing on the Technical Detail – that this chapter dives into – will help your players during their playing journeys over the years to come. It will also help them enjoy the game now!

Scanning

Scanning underpins everything that a player does, both with the ball and without the ball.

In possession, players are looking for their teammates, opposition players, space to exploit, and the goal.

Out of possession, players are looking for their teammates, opposition players, space to deny the opposition, and their own goal.

The more a player scans, the slower the game will seem to them, and they will be able to make quicker decisions, both with and without the ball.

Short passing

This is where players make a quick, accurate pass over a short distance, typically less than 10 yards.

- Look at the ball, target, ball.
- Non-kicking foot to the side and level with the ball.
- Strike the ball with the inside of the foot.
- Ankle locked.

- Strike through the centre of the ball to stop the ball from bobbling.

- The striking foot follows through in the direction the ball is aimed.

- Body upright, with head and knee over the ball.

- Passing factors: accuracy, weight, timing, disguise.

Lofted passing

This technique is useful when a player needs to lift the ball into the air over a distance. It is often used to bypass an opponent or change the direction of play.

- Look at the ball, target, ball.

- Non-kicking foot to the side and slightly behind the ball.

- Strike the ball with the instep or laces.

- Ankle locked.

- Strike the bottom third of the ball to get height.

- The striking foot follows through in the direction the ball is aimed.

- Body leaning back slightly, to help loft the ball.

- Passing factors: accuracy, weight, timing, disguise.

Swerve passing

This is where the ball curves in its trajectory due to the way it is struck with the outside of the foot.

- Look at the ball, target, ball.
- Angled approach to the ball.
- Non-kicking foot away and slightly behind the ball.
- Strike the ball with the outside or inside of the foot (nearer toes).
- Aim to strike the outside third of the ball.
- Wrap the foot around the ball for a longer contact.
- Passing factors: accuracy, weight, timing, disguise.

Driven passing

A driven pass is a powerful, ground-level pass that travels a long distance.

- Look at the ball, target, ball.
- Straight or slightly angled approach to the ball.
- Non-kicking foot alongside the ball.
- Strike the ball with the laces.
- Strike through the middle of the ball.
- Straight follow-through.
- Passing factors: accuracy, weight, timing, disguise.

Chip passing

This is where the ball is kicked with the toe or instep, lifting the ball into the air.

- Look at the ball, target, ball.
- Straight approach to the ball.
- Non-kicking foot close to the striking foot.
- Stab at the underneath of the ball with a straight foot.
- No follow-through.
- Passing factors: accuracy, weight, timing, disguise.

Receiving

Receiving refers to a player taking possession of the ball from a teammate's pass.

- Have a scan before the pass is made.
- Watch the ball as it arrives.
- If you have time, have another scan before receiving.
- Get in line with the ball.
- Decide which surface or body part to receive with.
- Relax on contact with the ball.
- Decide on the length of touch, depending on what is around you (space, teammates, opposition players).

Dribbling

Dribbling is the skill of moving the ball while running, keeping possession and avoiding opponents, using small touches and 1v1 skills.

- Have a positive attitude.

- Dribble at pace when possible.

- Small touches so that the ball is close.

- Use a change of pace when dribbling.

- Use both feet (inside/inside) or one foot (inside/outside).

- Use body feints to unbalance opposition players.

- Keep the ball on the safe side, away from defenders.

- Get head up to make the right decision of when to beat a player, and when to release the ball.

Running with the ball

Running with the ball refers to a player moving at speed, using big touches to exploit space.

- Have a positive attitude.

- Run with the ball at pace.

- Big touches to exploit space in front.

- Use the outside or inside of the foot (nearer toes) to control the ball.

- Keep the ball on the safe side, away from approaching defenders.

- Get head up to make the right decision when getting close to a defender.

Finishing

This refers to scoring goals, particularly with skill and precision, either inside or outside the box.

- Get head up to see the goalkeeper's position.
- If taking more than one touch, get the last touch out of feet to give space to strike the ball.
- Select the right surface of the foot to strike the ball with (depending on distance, angle, surrounding players).
- Pick where you want to finish.
- Follow through in the same direction to keep accuracy.
- Be ready for rebounds inside the box.

1v1 skills

These are techniques used by attackers to beat a defender in a 1v1 situation.

Here are some 1v1 skills that our players can learn. Searching them on YouTube is a great way to see them and break them down.

- Step over
- Flip flap
- Roulette
- Ronaldo Chop
- The Cut

- Scissors
- Matthews
- McGeady Spin
- La Croqueta

Types of turn

These are a variety of techniques a player uses to change direction, often to gain space, evade a defender, or maintain possession of the ball.

Here are some 1v1 skills that our players can learn. Once again, searching them on YouTube is an effective way to see and share them.

- L turn
- Inside hook turn
- Outside hook turn
- Cruyff turn
- Stepover turn
- Drag back turn
- Stop turn
- Step round turn

Creating and using space

Creating and using spaces is about a player's ability to move into areas away from opposition players and teammates.

- Regularly scan to recognise what is around, and where there is space to move into.

- Make sure that a player moves so that a teammate in possession can see their feet, giving them a passing option.

- Move away from defenders into a position where the defender can't see them 'going dark'.

- Look to receive beyond opposition players when possible.

- Make double movements to create space (go to show, show to go).

FA 2 and 3-player core moves

The FA 2 and 3-player moves are a great way to look at moments in the game which involve your players.

They are also a good way to start using terminology for these moves early on, so that players get to understand them and can communicate with each other when using them on the pitch.

2-player moves

Diagonal pass, straight run

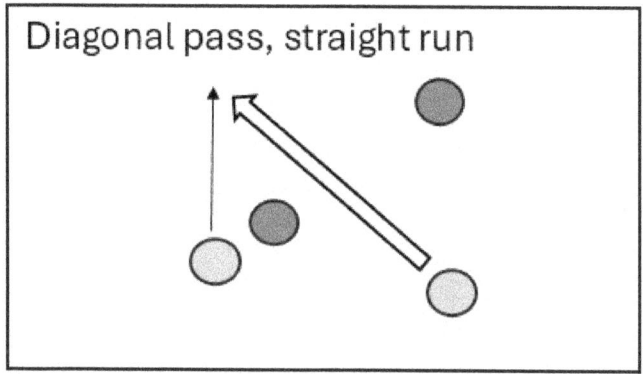

Straight run, diagonal run

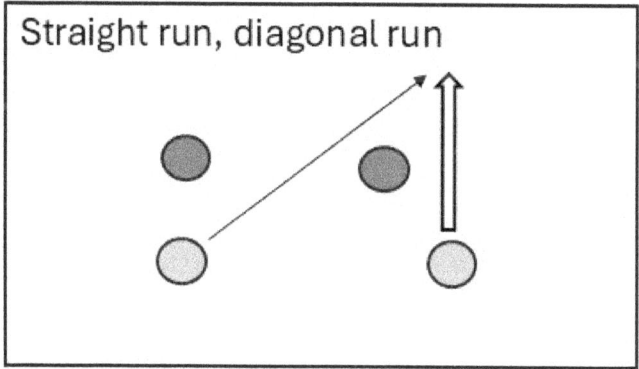

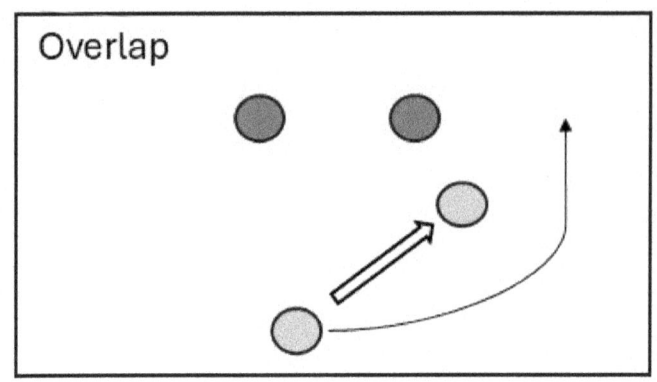

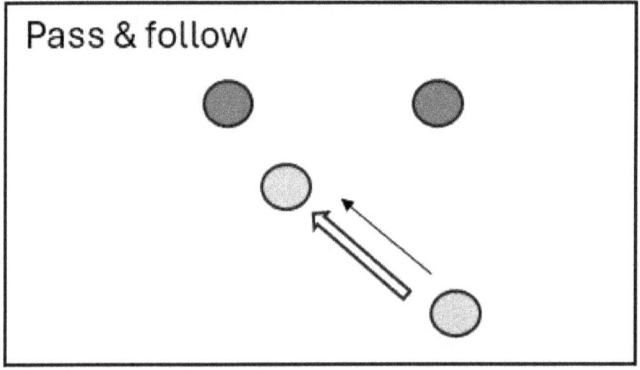

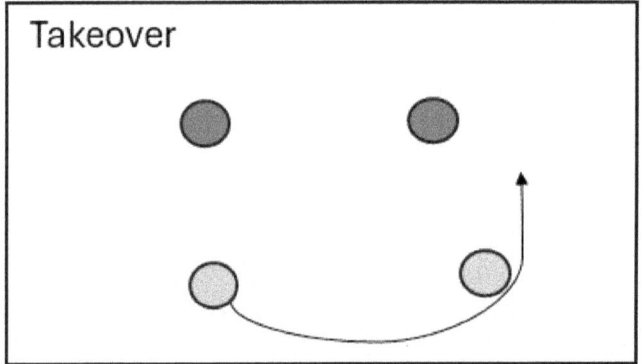

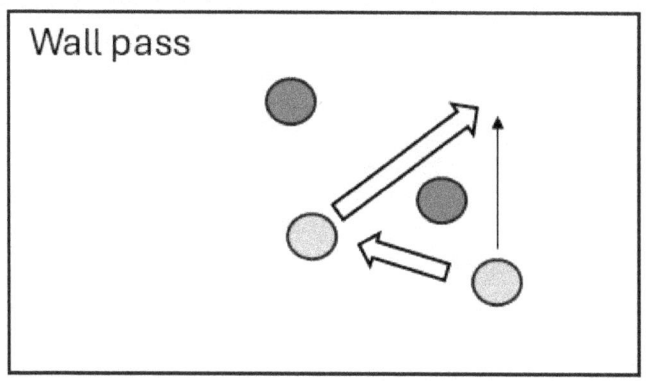

3-player moves

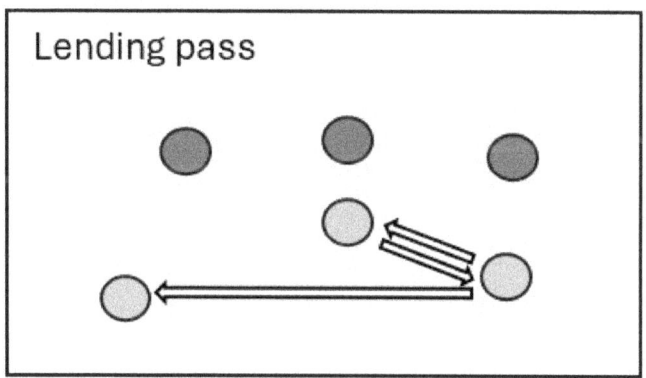

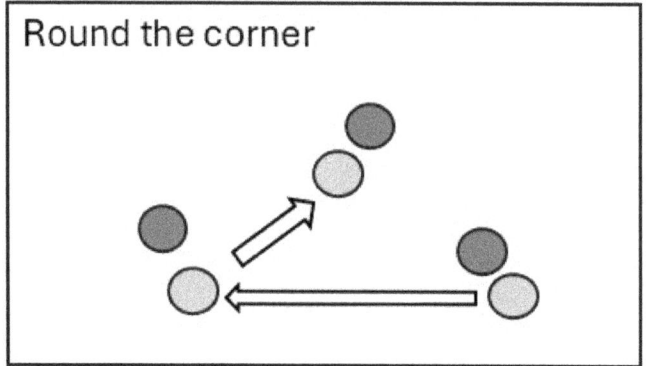

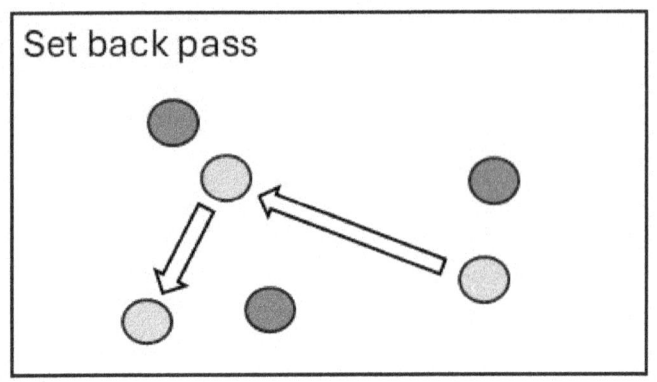

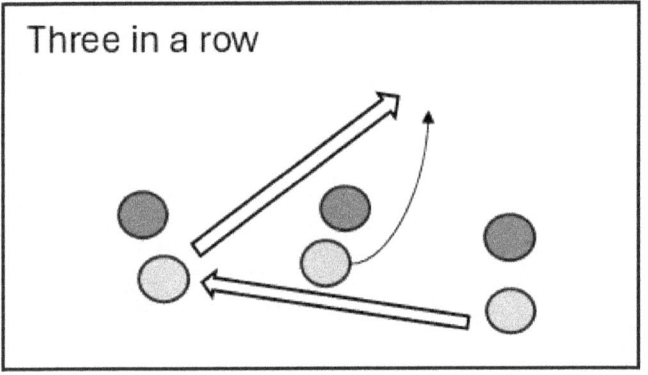

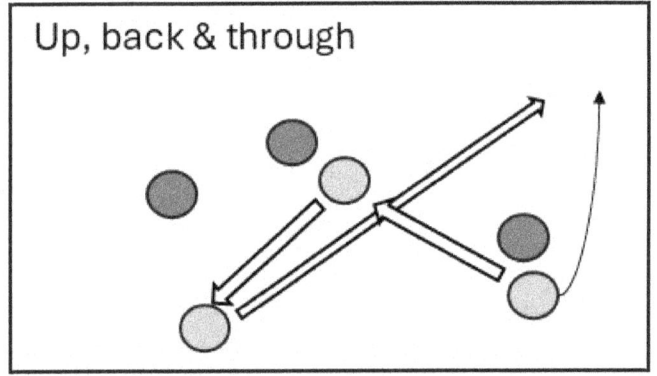

1v1 defending

This is a situation where one defender is tasked with stopping a single opposition player who has the ball.

- Intensity to close the opposition player down.
- Slow down when approaching the player.
- Use a split stance body shape (halfway between square on and side on).
- Show the opposition player towards the sideline or onto their non-dominant foot.
- Get low.
- Weight on balls of feet.
- Ball in line with back foot.
- Show patience (not diving in).
- Tackle using front foot.
- Use body and limbs.
- Stay on feet and avoid slide tackling when possible.

2v2 defending

2v2 defending is a situation where two defenders are tasked with stopping two opposition players – one who has the ball and another player who is close to them.

- Nearest player closes down the opposition player with the ball.

- Correct 1v1 defending technique from the nearest defender.

- Second defender positions to cover (distance and angle).

- Seesaw movement when the ball gets passed.

- Recovery run – goalside of the ball – if beaten.

- Communication.

Defending outnumbered

This is a situation where the defending team has fewer players in a particular area of the pitch than the opposition team.

- Look to delay the attack to allow teammates to recover.

- When possible, force the player on the ball wide.

- Stay between the ball and the goal.

- Look to turn an overload into a 1v1 by positioning. Potentially intercept a pass and turn the situation into a 1v1.

- Recovering defenders look to potentially back press to win the ball if possible. If not, look to recover into a supporting position.

7: Match Days

Giving equal minutes on match days

A lot of Foundation Phase coaches fall into the trap of playing their 'stronger players' more on match days and giving their 'weaker players' only a few minutes. Their need to win games takes over, and it shouldn't.

There are a few key things to consider. Firstly, players can make big leaps in development during the Foundation Phase, but if they aren't given a chance, players won't develop. They certainly won't develop by standing and watching the game.

As we go up from 5v5 to 11v11, we will need more players to start, and if those players haven't been playing as much, the whole team will struggle.

We may think that winning games and trophies in the Foundation Phase is important, and every child wants to win, but games should be viewed as a chance to develop our players.

In the Foundation Phase, scores aren't shown, nor are league tables published, as the main focus should be on development. When teams get to the Youth Development phase and above, there is plenty of time to focus more on results.

Rotating players' positions on match days

Earlier in the book, we discussed the value of rotating positions. It is important that we rotate positions on match days as well as during training sessions. It is easy to fall into the trap of focusing on winning the game, and playing players in what we think are currently their strongest positions. But match days are the perfect challenge for players to play in different positions. Over the long term, having a group of well-rounded players will benefit the team's results after the Foundation Phase, when teams are playing for leagues and cups.

Team talks

When working with Foundation Phase players, the two keys to team talks are simplicity and positivity. For young players, a match day is going to be challenging enough without us overloading them with masses of tactical information. Keep it simple and only focus on a few key pieces of information. Whether we are winning, drawing, or losing, Foundation Phase players don't need their coach to be negative or frustrated with them. Keep your communication and coaching positive, especially in difficult situations.

Team talks shouldn't be all about the coaches; they should be an opportunity for players to talk and give their feedback to the coaches. At half-time, and after the game, give the players some time to talk, then the players can give us their feedback before we start to talk. You will be surprised by what they come up with.

Linking training to match days

Rather than focusing on our team talks and coaching tactics or trying to cover everything, focus on the topic and coaching points from the previous training session. It will help you to narrow your focus.

Setting up match day objectives on a whiteboard that you can go through with your players before the game, and refer back to while the game is going on (as well as at half-time, and after the match) can help coaches and players.

For example, if the previous session was focused on 1v1 defending, you could set up three objectives on the board, focusing on:

- Intensity to close the opposition player down

- Slowing down when you get close

- Using a split stance body shape (halfway between square on and side on)

Pre-match warm-ups

A pre-match warm-up for a Foundation Phase team does not need to look like a pre-match warm-up you see with a First Team. The players don't need a highly structured routine or dynamic stretching. Think of your pre-match warm-ups as an extension of your practices; they are a great chance to continue working on the outcomes from the last session, and link in with the match day objectives you set.

Another pre-match warm-up to avoid is line drill shooting, where the whole squad is lined up, and they take turns having a shot at the goalkeeper. In the colder months, it means lots of players standing around waiting and getting cold. Plus, it is time when players could be getting lots of touches on the ball in a practice where everyone is involved.

Opposition coaches and officials

How you treat opposition officials is important in more ways than you would think. Most of the time, being respectful will be reciprocated by opposition coaches and officials, making the match day experience more enjoyable for everyone. Looking at the bigger picture, coaches and officials talk to each other, and we start to gain a reputation. That reputation should be as a respectful coach, not as a coach who is rude or argumentative.

Unfortunately, even in the Foundation Phase, you will come across some coaches or officials who are rude or argumentative. When that happens, the best thing you can do is not engage with them; don't escalate the situation... remain calm and respectful.

Foundation Phase formations

Although formations are secondary to technical detail, it is still good to pick a formation and stick to it so that players start to understand their relationships with each other on the pitch.

Which formation you use is a personal preference, but a good tip is to work back from the 11-a-side formation you want to eventually play, and use formations that link to it.

For example:

- 1-4-3-3 at 11v11
- 1-4-3-1 at 9v9
- 1-2-3-1 at 7v7
- 1-1-2-1 at 5v5

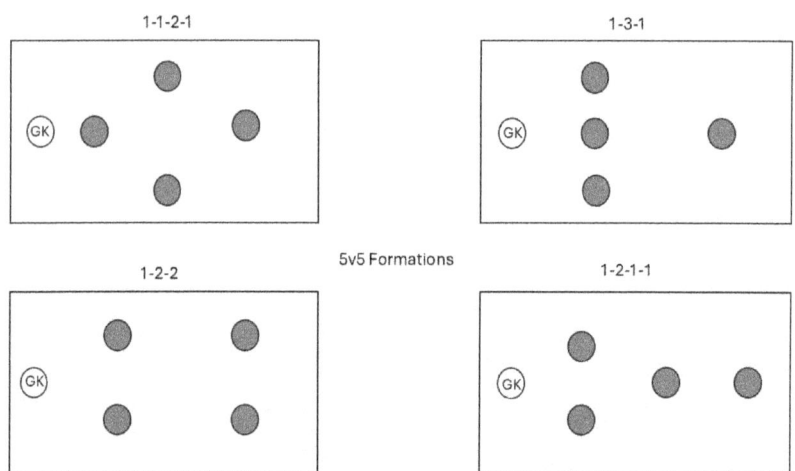

5v5 Formations

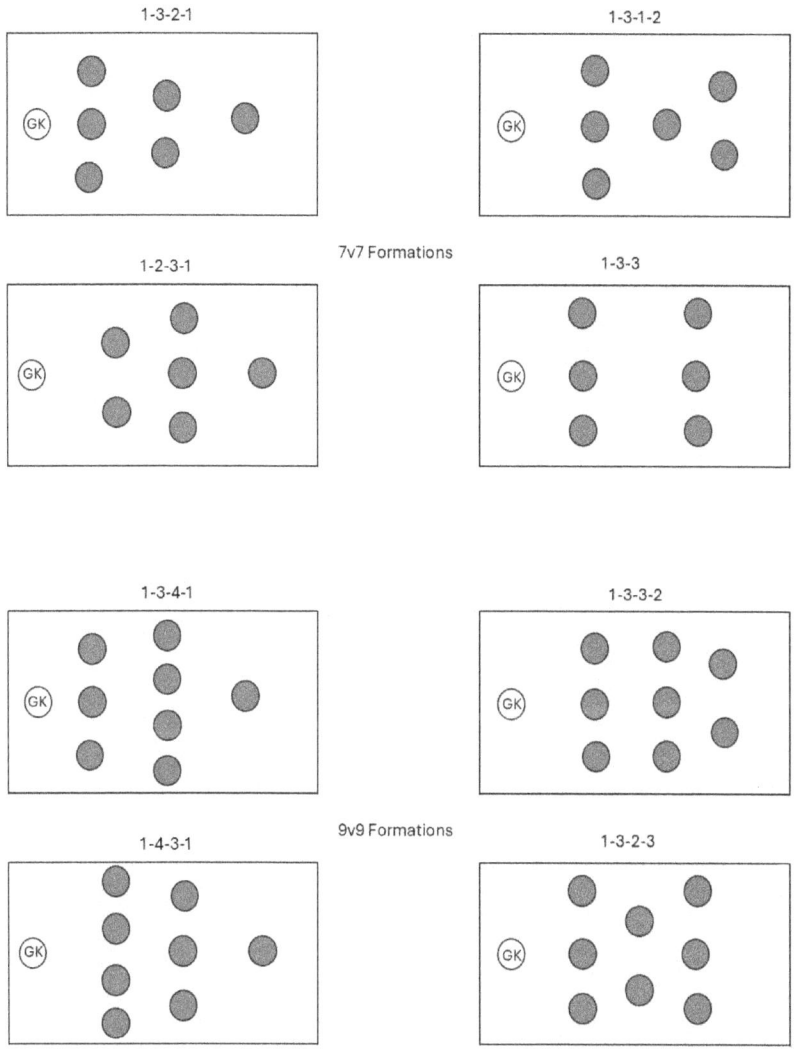

Reflecting on match days

Match days are a great opportunity to improve yourself and your players by reflecting after the game. Think about how you coached, what worked well, and what you could have done differently with your coaching. This will help you to become a more effective coach for your players. Also, think about your players' performances, as it will help you gain a better understanding of what *they* need to work on as individuals and as a group.

One tip would be not to reflect straight after a game. Reflecting a few hours or a day after the game is far more effective, as any emotion after the game has gone, and you can reflect with a more objective perspective.

*

Over the course of this book, I hope that you have picked up some great information that you might not find on coaching courses, as well as useful resources to take away and apply. Some main points to keep in mind are:

- The importance of creating a positive environment.

- The power of a high tempo and ball rolling time.

- The fact that positional rotation and equal minutes will help create long-term success.

- That enjoyment should be a high priority in the Foundation Phase.

- Technical detail is more important than tactics, and you now have the detail needed to help your players develop.

So, there you have it. I wish you all the very best in your coaching journey!

Rob

Other Books from The Publisher

"I have always struggled with session planners. They never include the sections I need, or the space to write and draw what I want."

The Bearded Coach's Football Session Planner

Football coach and coach educator Peter Prickett was frustrated with existing planners, so he decided to develop his own. Created for grassroots football coaches right through to professionals alike, it is structured around Peter's insights and knowledge of best practice, and addresses key session aims, including: What structure am I going to use for this session? What questions will I ask of my players? How can I challenge the whole group, units, and individuals?

Incorporating detailed guidance on how to get the most out of the planner (including context, principles of play, intervention methods, session format, and more), alongside example plans to help kickstart planning, 40 blank templates are provided for you to create your own sessions. This A4 soft-cover planner uses high-quality paper and a wire-bound binding so it can be folded flat, and each template comprises two facing pages, creating an A3 working area, so the whole session can be viewed – in detail – at once.

Whether you are an occasional coach or developing teams full-time, *The Bearded Coach's Football Session Planner* is a vital tool in your armoury for delivering high-quality training sessions.

Coaching Youth Football: What Soccer Coaches Can Learn From The Professional Game

Coaching Youth Football is the highly-anticipated follow-up to the international, best-selling soccer coaching book, *Making The Ball Roll*, by Ray Power.

With the help of dozens of contributors from across the professional, academy, and grassroots games, Ray delves into the art and science of coaching youth football players, using up-to-date studies, methods, and examples across 360 superb pages.

Coaching Youth Football covers the breadth of the game with compelling specifics, and with illustrations from across the football world – bringing together research, stories, best-practice, and a lifetime of experiences within the game. Chapters cover: Long-Term Player Development, Team Building, Modern Playing Positions, Age-Appropriate Coaching, Football Fitness, Small-Sided Games, Growth Mindset, Footballing Intelligence, Tactics, Coach Reflection, and more.

Maximise Your Training Sessions: Football Practices for Ever-Changing Numbers and Spaces

Have you ever planned the perfect football training session only to find half your players have failed to turn up? Or that your training area has been moved at the last minute, and you're now in half the space? Help is at hand!

Maximise Your Training Sessions is a book for coaches who are looking to design practical and meaningful practices for all coaching situations – whatever last-minute issues get thrown at them.

In this book, Rob McKay – Head Coach of Women's Football for the University of Manchester – goes through all the things a coach needs to consider before putting on an effective session: from space to players to equipment, right down to the weather! At the same time, it provides an in-depth look at how to create your own principles of play to produce quality and relevant coaching points for your practices.

More than 45 illustrated practices are included, and all of them are designed to be adjustable for player numbers, space, and set-up time.

This practical guide is perfect for both grassroots and experienced coaches looking to enhance their practice design and take their sessions to the next level.

Some of our 35+ soccer coaching books

www.BennionKearny.com/soccer

www.ingramcontent.com/pod-product-compliance
Lightning Source LLC
Chambersburg PA
CBHW050033090426

42735CB00022B/3466